THE KIDS ARE ALL LEFT

ALSO BY DAVID FARIS

IT'S TIME TO FIGHT DIRTY: HOW
DEMOCRATS CAN BUILD A LASTING MAJORITY
IN AMERICAN POLITICS

THE KIDS ARE ALL

LEFT

How Young Voters Will Unite America

DAVID FARIS

MELVILLE HOUSE
BROOKLYN • LONDON

THE KIDS ARE ALL LEFT

First published in 2020 by Melville House Publishing
Copyright © David Faris, 2019
All rights reserved
First Melville House Printing: June 2020

Melville House Publishing   Suite 2000
46 John Street   and   16/18 Woodford Road
Brooklyn, NY 11201   London E7 0HA

mhpbooks.com
@melvillehouse

ISBN: 978-1-61219-820-0
ISBN: 978-1-61219-821-7 (eBook)

Library of Congress Catalog Number: 2020932928

Designed by Beste M. Doğan

Printed in the United States of America
1 3 5 7 9 10 8 6 4 2

A catalog record for this book is available from the Library of Congress

*For my sweet, beautiful Anoush and
the world I hope to leave you*

CONTENTS

THE REPUBLICAN PARTY IS SCREWED

PICTURE YOURSELF FOR a moment as the commissioner of Major League Baseball, tasked with guarding the fortunes and traditions of the national pastime. You are in Kansas City's Kaufmann Stadium on a long, languid, humid summer afternoon enjoying a hot dog and a Boulevard Tropical Pale Ale when one of your newest underlings, an adorably awkward math major fresh out of MIT, plops down into the seat next to you with some alarming news. "Our fan base is quickly dying," he says. He shows you a thick binder full of data that confirms your worst fears, the sort of worries you'd prefer to set aside while enjoying the Royals-Tigers game unfolding in front of you. Most of baseball's hard-core fans—the ones who buy tickets for the games, pay $150 a month for their monthly cable subscription to catch tilts on TV, and spend their free time in fantasy leagues full of their college friends—are over fifty. Americans under thirty, especially in growing demographics like Latinx fans, are choosing soccer or basketball over baseball.

The underling is blunt. "In twenty years, we will be ice hockey," he warns, a sport intensely beloved by a tiny minority but mostly ignored by the larger culture. "In twenty more, we'll be boxing."

He hands you a bullet-pointed list of ways to address this problem, refuses your offer of a beer (young people aren't drinking much these days, after all), and walks away.

Instead of doing the sensible thing and following his advice, like ramping up youth league efforts, financing under-served communities, quickening the game's pace, promoting the sport's diverse stars, and perhaps placing major-league franchises in Cuba, the Dominican Republic, and other places where baseball remains wildly popular, you make a stunning gamble by doubling down on the sport's core, dying demographic of older white men. You instruct teams to hold "Caucasian Nights" celebrating white culture. You eliminate wild-card playoff games, pitch clocks, and designated hitters to return to "tradition." You lobby the government to make it harder for international players to get visas, and you appoint old white dudes with thready pulses and gray faces to every single important position of leadership in the game. You ban Latin American players from wearing jewelry or getting tat-toos that represent their countries of origin. You look at the hordes of older white fans driving in from the exurbs and packing stadium after stadium, and the wall-to-wall media coverage of your antics and bask in self-satisfaction. You suddenly have a million followers on Twitter, most of whom aren't even baseball fans but rather people who seem to enjoy human suffering. Baseball gets a little dead-cat bounce, but the future still looks grim.

If betting on a dying core demographic, deliberately alienating young people, and delighting in open, unapologetic racism seems like a total genius move to you, you're going to love the strategy of the contemporary Republican Party in the United States. There's really no way to sugarcoat this: the GOP is getting clobbered so badly in the competition for young voters that the party's future looks bleaker than an episode of *The Handmaid's Tale*. The MIT grad has been sitting next to party leaders for years now, reading exit polls and surveys and results in election after election, warning about the extinction-level political event hurtling their way to no avail. The chimerical "victory" of Donald Trump in the 2016 election and his transformation of the Republican Party from the—wink-wink—super-secret electoral home of America's racists to an open, frothing white power organization with fond linkages to every authoritarian, right-wing nationalist group on the planet has momentarily rescued the GOP from its demographic destiny. The Trump era has given hope to reactionaries who have long dreamed of reimposing their vision of white, male dominance on the country, and legitimacy to a long list of far-right crackpots who once operated at the margins of society. And if Trump and the Republicans were polling ahead, or even respectably, with young people, I'd be genuinely worried as I scroll through property listings in Ontario.

But they aren't. Even as the US economy hummed along with its lowest levels of unemployment in forty years, as the stock market reached new heights, the Republican Party remains about as popular as tooth extraction with everyone under the age of forty. They see America as a society dominated by conservatives since their parents were children, and blame baby boomers and Gen Xers for systematically looting the country and burning down the bridges that once led to success and prosperity immediately after crossing them. Once upon a time, you could pursue affordable higher education for next to nothing, support a family, and buy a house with a few years of hard work and savings. Now, you have to take out fifty grand in crippling loans just to get through college, even at many flagship state universities that were once effectively free, and the world that confronts you when you get out is harrowing. The best jobs are in major cities, where everything feels up-charged. Real wages in many industries haven't increased in decades, and more and more of your limited income gets eaten up by health care costs and housing, even as your callous elders mock you for the avocado toast and lattes that you can't afford and don't buy anyway.

Worse, too many people over the age of forty-five seem not to get it. They don't understand why they can't call you "hot lips" anymore or make jokes about Polish people or imitate foreign accents, and they are outraged at the idea of a woman being the lead in the new James Bond movie, and they think older brothers and dads exist to protect the virtue of young women, and they quietly (or not-so-quietly since the election of Trump) believe that the plight of poor folks and minorities is their own fault because they don't work hard enough and that young people are "snowflakes" who were given participation trophies just for showing up and whose brains were warped in childhood by parents who told them how special they were and that kids should know what the world is really like and that most of them are not special at all and they should not be told fairy tales about equality and justice, and they are tired of having their Thanksgiving soliloquies about Ronald Reagan ruined by the sour attitudes of their kid's punk social justice warrior girlfriend or boyfriend, and they have nothing against Muslims or Africans—they were nice to one of them just last week!—but they think it's all gone too far, and that somewhere soon they are going to encounter a transgender Syrian activist in the bathroom and that, *that*, that's why they voted for Trump, and even though sometimes he should shut up on Twitter and stop whining, everything he is doing is basically fine and overdue, and maybe the kids will understand someday, even if they don't now. It's all for their own good.

Well, the reality is that, every minute, about twenty people who think like that draw their final breath and expire, and then they are simultaneously replaced in the eligible voting pool by an eighteen-year-old with a Democratic Socialists of America, or DSA, membership and a *Jacobin* subscription and an unsustainably high college tuition bill and in the general population by another baby that will have something like a 67 percent chance of growing up to be a leftist. The basic dynamic is a Republican Party increasingly dominated by and aligned with a dying white demographic and a Democratic Party that is not exactly beloved but is grudgingly supported come election time by overwhelming majorities of young people who haven't yet voted in numbers sufficient enough to make anyone take notice. And it is in the process of transforming our politics in ways long dreamed about by Democratic strategists and theorists, whose visions of "demographic destiny" may be accelerated by the galloping stupidity, insufferable, unearned arrogance, and legendary incompetence of the Trump administration.

That American politics is on the verge of a major disruption is, and should be, pretty hard to believe. The United States has been described for decades as "closely divided" politically, and the description today is still quite apt. Neither party's candidate has won more than 53 percent of the vote in a presidential election since 1988. Three of the past four presidents have taken office after winning less than 50 percent of the vote. Attitudes are so hardened that the correlation of voting outcomes in states from one presidential election to the next is extraordinarily high. The country has been so closely divided for so long that wild and dramatic swings from Democrats to Republicans and back in midterm elections are the norm rather than the exception. Neither party seems to get more than five minutes to govern before a pitchfork-wielding rage mob shows up to toss them out of office at the very next election. Just as it seemed like one party was consolidating its grip on power, as when Republicans won their third straight presidential election in 1988, or when Democrats swept to power in back-to-back landslides in 2006 and 2008, or when Republicans captured Congress and the presidency in 2016, the bottom dropped out, and the seemingly doomed party staged an improbable comeback that looked much more predictable in hindsight. A thousand eulogies for the dead and dying Democratic and Republican parties have been proven, again and again, to be wrong. The dreams of consultants and strategists all end in the same nightmare of watching your recently vanquished opponents rise from the dead and smite you.

Today's Republican Party, however, is doing its best to break this thirty-year-long stalemate in American politics—not by expanding its appeal and picking off pieces of the Democratic coalition, but by systematically repulsing and alienating America's youngest voters. The way that the American political system so often fails to translate majority sentiment into majority governing coalitions has falsely convinced GOP elites that their popularity is growing, rather than shrinking, and it is causing the those who do understand the problem to engage in democracy-warping escalations to protect their ill-gotten power.

Others simply assume that the pendulum will eventually swing back with toward young folkspeople and that today's DSA radicals will be tomorrow's Not In My Backyard old people fighting to preserve single-family zoning and voting, reluctantly, for the people who promise to take less of their hard-earned money on tax day. Most analysts in the popular press are missing the significance of this trend by assuming that young voters have always skewed liberal, only to drift into curmudgeonly conservatism as they age. They'll fumble around for some version of "If you're not a liberal at twenty-five, you have no heart and if you're not a conservative at thirty-five you have no brain" and think about that one family member who volunteered for George McGovern only to become an old person proudly drinking out of a MAGA mug every morning and plotting to leave his grandchildren a planet completely obliterated by global warming.

This is simply not true on many different levels. First of all, young people have not always voted for Democrats and have not always leaned left, let alone by the margins we see today. Ronald Reagan won the youngest voting demographic by 22 points in 1984, and in 1988, George H. W. Bush edged out Michael Dukakis with them by 6 points. In 1992, Bill Clinton did better with elderly voters than he did with the youngest. As recently as 2000, Republican George W. Bush tied Democrat Al Gore with eighteen-to-twenty-four-year-olds, according to exit polls.[1] Young people in the polling era have never been especially conservative, in comparison to the rest of the population, but nor have they been as heavily left as most people think.

Something unprecedented started happening in 2002. In an unusually strong midterm election for the sitting president's party, the GOP picked up seats in both the House and Senate. But according to exit polls, Democrats won eighteen-to-twenty-nine-year-olds by 2 points. That was the last time Republicans came within single digits of winning the country's youngest voters in the national House vote. Democrats won eighteen-to-twenty-nine-year-olds by 12 points in 2004, 22 in 2006, 30 in 2008, 16 in 2010, 22 in 2012, 10 in 2014, 14 in 2016, and then by a mind-boggling 35 points in 2018. Several of these elections were Republican wave years, particularly 2010 and 2014—total disasters for Democrats amid a very real backlash against the Obama administration. Still, young voters barely budged.

2018 was a wave election year, of course, and Democrats should not necessarily expect to win younger voters by these margins every year. But there should have been two things that terrified Republican elites in President Trump's first (and hopefully only) midterm election. The virtually unheard-of blowout with young people is one. The second is that the young voters who broke decisively away from the Republican Party starting in 2004 have become the thirty-to-forty-four age bracket, and their views are pretty much unchanged.

Democrats won this group, a mix of millennials and younger Gen Xers, by 19 points. Through marriage and child-rearing and home-buying and all of the material trappings of early middle age that most people assume turn you into conservatives, these voters remained Democratic, with no tangible statistical evidence that the GOP was making inroads with them. So it's not just today's kids who are all left. It's elder millennials and younger Gen Xers. The only thing holding Republican power together in 2019 is the fact that older voters turn out in substantially higher numbers than younger ones.

What was so shocking about the continued Democratic dominance of young Americans in 2016 and 2018 is that ordinarily you would expect new voters, at some point, to rebel against the party in power and embrace ideological alternatives to the status quo. Despite losing governorships across the country, bleeding out thousands of state legislative seats and then handing Congress and the presidency to Republicans at the conclusion of the Obama era, Democrats never lost young people, not even for a moment. In fact, if only people under the age of twenty-nine had voted in 2016, Hillary Clinton would have been elected by Reagan-Mondale margins in the Electoral College. And while this book will be published prior to the 2020 election and will steadfastly refuse to offer a prediction about what the ultimate outcome will be, you can be highly confident that the Democratic nominee will beat Donald Trump by at least 25 points with eighteen-to-twenty-nine-year-olds. In fact, a 25-point deficit with that demographic would, in the upside-down universe of Trumpism where the president brags about 49 percent approval ratings on Twitter, be considered a kind of accomplishment.

The short story is that the Republican Party is well and completely screwed if they don't start making inroads with young voters, people of color, and women—and soon. The longer story is an attempt to explain how, for almost two decades and counting, young people have been moving politically left and staying there, and to think about how this trend, if it continues (and it looks like it will), might blow apart the long stalemate in American politics and either force the GOP to the left or consign it to a generation as a distinct national minority party. Either of these outcomes, frankly, would be just fine, although watching the Republican Party come apart in fiery ruins like the Hindenburg would be extremely satisfying for everyone on the left. Starting in about 2024, the twenty-nine-year-old millennials who broke against George W. Bush will be nearing fifty.

Please don't mistake this book as a prediction that the Republican Party won't win another election for thirty years, as much as I would like that to be true. While it would be awesome to get hate-cited for the rest of my life as the pre-eminent example of a Very Wrong Argument, I feel obligated to issue the standard caveats that the reviewers will probably ignore and that Sean Hannity's research staff almost certainly won't read. Today's heavily Republican forty-five-to-sixty-four-year-olds are going to be around for a disturbingly long time, lingering like a wind-lashed Midwestern winter, voting for whoever Tucker Carlson tells them to (or perhaps for Tucker Carlson himself), likely clinging to life long enough for them to see their property investments in the Outer Banks of North Carolina and Miami Beach made valueless by rising seas and maybe even long enough to see the person they've been made to fear the most in the whole world by the Fox News grifters, let's say Alexandria Ocasio-Cortez, elected to two terms as president.

Like all elderly people with nothing better to do, they will stagger out to vote in massive numbers, and sometimes it will be enough for them to win. The fact that as you read this, Democrat Doug Jones is a US senator from Alabama and that Massachusetts—*Massachusetts!*—recently reelected a Republican governor by 33 points in 2018 should be a reminder that anything is possible in politics. Even if Democrats win the next four presidential elections, Republicans will likely win the House or Senate frequently enough that it won't always feel like we've entered a new era of Democratic dominance in national politics. And of course, Democrats could take total power in 2020 or 2024 and get left holding the bag for another recession, the unfortunate position they found themselves in after Barack Obama's election in 2008. Or they could inflict some genuinely unfortunate policy on the country—perhaps by putting the Modern Monetary Theorists (don't even ask) who are still on the ideological fringe in charge of the US economy—that finally breaks the party's nearly two-decade hold on young folks.

But for now, the kids are all left. They've been marching left for twenty years with no real end in sight. Which end of this trend would you rather be on? The bad news for the GOP is that everything we know about how people make voting choices and form partisan preferences suggests that most of today's young Democrats will turn into middle-age Democrats and then elderly Democrats before becoming dead Democrats. The tougher, sit-down-and-brace-yourself news for the red team is that most of these young lefties will shun dating-pool-eligible Republicans—if they even know any—and marry one another and then have a bunch of blue diaper babies, who will outnumber their Republican counterparts even more decisively than they do now. Every iteration of this demographic nightmare will look worse for Republicans unless and until they change their policies, abandon white supremacism, and embrace this country's multicultural destiny.

I wouldn't wait by the phone for that one.

How did we get here, to the precipice of a long period of Democratic domination of national politics? After all, it hasn't been that long since Beltway pundits were throwing around the phrase "center-right nation," Democrats were hopelessly buried in the minority nationally, and Republicans were aglow with their best showing in a national election since the 1980s.

That was just sixteen years ago. The Democratic Party was at one of its most depressing post-war nadirs. Republicans, led by President George W. Bush, had gleefully and successfully weaponized the pervasive climate of fear and paranoia in the aftermath of 9/11, winning a rare and decisive midterm victory in 2002 for the incumbent president and seemingly settling in for a long stay in power. And as bad as that seemed, things would get worse in 2004, with Bush edging out Democratic nominee John Kerry for re-election and Republicans expanding their House and Senate majorities. With the war in Iraq already having turned sour by election day, the outcome was a tremendous shock to Democrats, many of whom simply could not believe that they had lost to the tongue-tied Bush again. Commentators claimed incessantly that America was a center-right nation. Reporters Tom Hamburger and Peter Wallsten wondered not long after, "So pervasive and durable is the Republicans' strength, it is time to ask: Is the United States becoming a one-party country?"[2]

But in 2002, a book-length pep talk for the left had dropped in the form of John Judis and Ruy Teixeira's *The Emerging Democratic Majority*, a self-conscious refiguring of Kevin Phillips's classic *The Emerging Republican Majority*, written in 1969, which correctly predicted a generation of Republican dominance of American national politics. Judis and Teixeira didn't waste any time getting to their thesis. "We believe that the Republican era Phillips presciently perceived in 1969 is over," they wrote. "We are witnessing the end of Republican hegemony."[3] For a book published two years before the Democrats' worst national electoral disaster since 1988, this was a bold thesis indeed.

Yet for long-suffering liberals still traumatized by the cliffhanger-turned-catastrophe of the 2000 election and the mysterious spell the hapless Bush had cast over the country, the book's central argument might as well have been injected directly into their arteries. Forget what looks like the party's miserable predicament at the moment, and look forward to a victorious coalition of college-educated professionals, African Americans, Latinx, they predicted. Democrats would rule "where the production of ideas and services has either redefined or replaced assembly-line manufacturing, particularly in the North and West, but also including some Southern states like Florida."[4] While they issued the standard caveats too (the same ones at the beginning of this book!), they claimed that "over the next decade, Democrats will enter elections at an advantage over the Republicans in securing a majority."

The big, leftist blogs of the period, including Josh Marshall's *Talking Points Memo*, the now-defunct *MyDD*, and *The Daily Kos*, gave the book extensive coverage. Judis and Teixeira's confident book, a bestseller, was so ubiquitous in Democratic circles that a crude simplification of its premise—"demography is destiny"—became a kind of data nerd's rallying cry for the next several electoral cycles. The proportion of whites in presidential electorates was in terminal, if achingly slow, decline, while the share of African Americans and Latinx was on the rise. If Democrats continued to win decisive majorities of these voters and to hold their own with whites, a new Democratic majority could indeed emerge. And when Democrats crushed Republicans in the 2006 midterm elections, seizing the House and Senate and then capturing towering majorities along with the presidency in 2008, Judis and Teixeira seemed vindicated. Democrats were confident that these victories would not be illusory. Republicans, one analyst predicted in 2010, were "unlikely to retake the majority in either chamber—not in these midterms or the ones that will follow."[5] Just before Obama's landslide victory, another writer, perhaps drunk on the possibility of long-sought dominance of American politics, mused that it was "the perfect time to crush contemporary conservatism without mercy and to enact the kind of progressive agenda that only sweeping power will allow" and urged Obama to "drop Republicanism over the ledge of a skyscraper and watch it plummet to its gruesome demise."[6]

Okay, fine, that was me. I've learned my lesson.[7]

We all know what happened next. First, the "emerging Democratic majority" was not distributed equally, much less ideally. The concentration of Democratic voters in big cities and metro areas and the disproportionate share of left-leaning voters in a small number of heavily Democratic states like California, Illinois, and New York made it much more difficult to maintain control of the House and Senate than people like Teixeira envisioned. And the young voters who propelled Obama's victory in 2008 dropped off the map in the critical midterm elections of 2010 and 2014, with turnout rates for millennials plummeting to levels not conducive to success for Democratic candidates nationwide. The strategist who can solve the youth-turnout problem could single-handedly usher in a long period of Democratic dominance. And while youth turnout is likely to be comparatively high in the 2020 presidential election, as observers expect record turnout, no serious analyst believes that young Americans will suddenly start turning out at the same rate as sixty-somethings.[8] There is, unfortunately, not much more we can do than wait for turnout rates for these left-leaning generations to catch up to those of their elders.

So, far from plummeting to its doom in the aftermath of Obama's sweeping triumph, the Republican Party quickly absolved itself of all responsibility for the Great Recession that started under its watch and set about ruthlessly opposing nearly everything President Obama proposed. After years of drunken spending on Bush's wars and tax cuts, GOP elites unabashedly reinvented themselves as deficit hawks and relentlessly chipped away at the kind of government spending that might have accelerated an economic recovery. Far from wiping out the strain of prejudice and resentment unleashed by Sarah Palinism—the cynical pitting of a mythical "real America" in the rural heartland against liberal elites and minorities in the cities—leading Republicans embraced her vision and paved the way for the rise of the demagogue who took over the party in 2016. Democrats got "shellacked" in the critical 2010 midterms, not only giving away their House majority, but losing control of the decennial redistricting process in so many states that Republicans locked in control of the House for eight long years and gerrymandered themselves into seemingly permanent state legislative majorities in places like North Carolina, Pennsylvania and even rapidly bluing Virginia.

The gruesome economic carnage of the recession spilled relentlessly into Obama's presidency, and voters disliked the financial stimulus package as well as the significant reform of the health care system ushered in by the Affordable Care Act. The benefits of both would become much clearer after 2010, but by then the House was gone, and Democrats were no longer able to achieve much at all through Congress. Voters in the rust belt quickly forgot that President Obama saved the auto industry and as many as one million jobs by presiding over nearly the entirety of a six-year, $80 billion bailout. Republican governors stymied the expansion of Medicaid and designed new voter suppression methods to drive down turnout from the Democratic coalition. And though Obama was reelected in 2012, he never again had Democratic control of Congress to pursue lasting policy reforms.

One additional raindrop on Ruy and Judis's parade is some ambiguity in the commonly accepted picture of demographic change in America, which might be a bit more complicated than it looked at first glance. It turns out that ethnic and racial identity is not static. Particularly as time goes on and the first generation becomes the third, certain kinds of immigrants may identify themselves as "white" to census-takers and perhaps start voting like they are white too—that is, overwhelmingly for Republicans. Because Latinx people are the fastest-growing minority population in America, if some substantial subset of self-identified Latinx suddenly decides to think of themselves as white and adopt that voting behavior, too, it could upset the predictions of a majority-minority America that have so roiled conservatives and struck fear into the hearts of white Americans. Donald Trump's better-than-expected performance with Latinx voters in 2016 can at least be partially attributed to changing self-identification.

To compound this problem, the design of the American political system is biased against the emerging Democratic coalition, in ways that are both intentional and unintentional. Take the United States Senate, for instance, which has been controlled since 2015 by Mitch McConnell and the Republican Party after the GOP wiped out nine Democratic seats in the 2014 wave election. If you add up the vote totals for Democrats and Republicans in 2014, 2016 and 2018—during which time all 100 seats were up for grabs (and then some if you count special elections)—Democratic candidates won 5.4 million more votes than Republican candidates, even if you take the vote totals for the losing candidates in California's Democrat-on-Democrat elections in 2016 and 2018 and hand them directly to the GOP. If the Senate were elected by popular vote, Democrats would have controlled it from 2017 through 2020. In the House, the story is similar—Democrats won the popular vote for the chamber in the 2012 presidential election, and only narrowly lost it in 2016, yet in both cases Republicans maintained enormous majorities. And of course, the presidency—a Republican candidate has only won the popular vote once since 1988, in 2004. The last two Republican presidents initially came into office with popular vote minorities. The GOP's grip on the presidency, the Senate, and the Courts are almost entirely products of an electoral system that awards more power to the political minority than it does to the political majority.

If you extend this logic all the way back to 2000, and count control of the presidency, House, and Senate as a single point in each electoral cycle, Republicans have won eighteen of thirty pieces of the federal government in the ten national elections held in the twenty-first century. But under a fair system in which the president is elected by a direct national vote, and the House and the Senate are controlled by whoever wins the most total votes, Democrats would have had a 19–11 advantage. To be clear, it's not that Democrats would have had unified control in DC nonstop since the turn of the century, but the narrative would have been quite different, and the policy outcomes would have been dramatically changed. For starters, a Democrat would have filled four of six Supreme Court vacancies since 2000 and would currently enjoy a 6–3 majority on the Supreme Court (assuming no Mitch McConnell seat-holding shenanigans). There would have been no

Bush tax cuts. Indeed, there would have been no George W. Bush, at least not as president. He would have joined Bob Dole and Walter Mondale in the glorious pantheon of losing major party candidates. There would have been no Iraq War, no Citizens United decision, no gutting of the Voting Rights Act, no Donald Trump. Democrats would have had another two years of unified control of the federal government from 2013 to 2015 and then again from 2019 to 2021. You might already be enrolled in a Medicare For All plan.[9]

	ACTUAL			FAIR SYSTEM		
	House	Senate	President	House	Senate	President
2000	R	R	R	R	D	D
2002	R	R	R	R	R	D
2004	R	R	R	R	D	R
2006	D	D	R	D	D	R
2008	D	D	D	D	D	D
2010	R	R	D	R	R	D
2012	R	D	D	D	D	D
2014	R	R	D	R	R	D
2016	R	D	R	R	D	D
2018	D	R	R	D	D	D

As Republicans never tire of pointing out, this is all theoretical, since the rules of the political system that the United States actually has are well known to both parties, if less so to voters themselves. But Teixeira's thesis might look quite different and have a totally different reputation if American election results were truly based on a one-person, one-vote system rather than the hodgepodge of antiquated and laughably indefensible practices that comprise the US electoral order. While President Trump claims, absurdly, that he would have won the popular vote if he had campaigned in California, for instance, there isn't much actual or theoretical evidence to suggest that results in the close elections of 2000, 2004, or 2016 would have looked much different, in terms of aggregate vote totals, without the Electoral College. What is true is that we would already be thinking of the early twenty-first century as a period of Democratic predominance of American politics rather than the sharply divided but GOP-leaning country that many people assume we live in. The point is that millennial voters have already brought massive change to the US political system. But this impact has been deadened by the institutions and therefore mostly missed by observers and analysts.

A few people here and there are starting to see the shape of what is to come. Last year, the conservative *New York Times* columnist David Brooks wrote an article about how young people were turning away from the Republican Party. He claimed, "it's hard to look at the generational data and not see long-term disaster for Republicans," citing election results from 2018, the smaller shares of whites in the millennial and Generation Z cohorts, as well as what appear to be their predominantly liberal ideological tendencies.[10] But as far as Brooks is concerned, this seems to have happened yesterday, instead of the nearly twenty-year-long trend that appears as though it will continue indefinitely. In Fall 2019, Democratic pollster Stanley Greenberg published *RIP GOP: How the New America Is Dooming the Republicans*. Greenberg is both too confident and too focused on the present, stating: "The year 2020 will produce a second blue wave on at least the scale of the first in 2018 and finally will crash and shatter the Republican Party that was consumed by the ill-begotten battle to stop the New America from governing."[11]

But they have the right idea. In the Trump-conquered circles of the new right, on the other hand, there is what can only be described as total denial. Many appear to believe that, as columnist Salena Zito wrote, "it is Donald Trump and the Republicans who have realigned American politics, by capturing Michigan, Wisconsin and Pennsylvania and thereby cracking the Democrats' so-called Blue Wall in 2016," and that the inroads made with white voters that year are just the leading edge of a larger knife that will further cut into Democratic majorities. The rebound in the total white vote between 2012 and 2016, for Zito and Todd, suggests that Trump's grip on American politics is not temporary and that the GOP can stay into power by becoming the party of the working class and dominating rural areas the way that Democrats have long swept the vote in big metro regions.[12] Zito and Todd's analysis misses several important developments in American politics, but none more so than the youth vote. Trump won 61 percent of the overall rural vote, according to exit polls, but only 53 percent with those under the age of thirty. This might seem like an insignificant difference, but it is the difference between winning and losing for the GOP. A Republican Party that wins rural areas by 20 points could see an extended period of dominance; one that wins by single digits, on the other hand, is probably doomed to the wilderness for the foreseeable future.

This will eventually have very dire consequences for Republicans. It looks like this: Republican voters now lean heavily male, religious, white, and older. Democrats dominate with voters of color, voters under forty-five, and voters who are unaffiliated religiously. Set aside for a second how much policy differences factor into these divisions versus how much we have been sorted into emotionally blinkered tribes thirsting for bare-knuckled political warfare. Given the US population that exists today, these splits probably give the GOP a fighting chance in the 2020 elections, but another four years of banking on this coalition will be ruinous.

The rest of this book will explain why this is happening. In chapter 1, I will describe the current and horrendous predicament of American politics—a sharply divided country, with political institutions that nevertheless systematically advantage the contemporary Republican Party over Democrats and have produced election outcomes and policy results far to the right of what the country seems to want. Mostly because of runaway hyperpartisanship from the Republican Party, and because control of the House, Senate, and presidency has flipped between Democrats and Republicans so frequently, major national problems have gone unaddressed since the turn of the century—or worse, have been badly exacerbated. Meanwhile, deepening hostility between the parties—what political scientists call *affective polarization*—has raised the stakes of every election, made politics look and feel nastier, and has led to fears of violence and civil war. But what if there were very clear signs that this era of legislative stalemate were coming to a close?

Chapter 2 takes a longer look at the growing iceberg drifting toward the Republican ship. What does it mean for young Americans to have voted decisively Democratic for the past eighteen years and counting? With each massive drubbing at the hands of the youngest voters, the GOP lengthens the knife that is cutting a swathe through its electoral fortunes. Republicans are now getting creamed with voters aged eighteen to forty-four. In twenty years, those voters will dominate the even more critical forty-five-to-sixty-four demographic, and there is no sign yet that the Republican Party is set to offset Democratic dominance with this cohort by winning incoming voters. What would American politics look like with one party dominating voters across generations?

In chapter 3, I will tackle one of the most persistent myths in American politics: the idea that young people have always been liberal but that some significant percentage turns conservative as they age, have families, and acquire larger stakes in the material world. While we don't have centuries of polling for confirmation, the data that we do have suggests overwhelmingly that your political beliefs as a young adult are likely to be your political beliefs for the rest of your life. This chapter will explore the scholarship on party identification and "inherited partisanship," making it clear that there is no massive set of late-in-life political transformations waiting to save the Republican Party from doom. It will also offer some insight into other factors that shape partisanship and why most of those influences are working against the Republican Party today. The bottom line: if the GOP doesn't start winning young people when they are young, they will consign the party to minority status for a generation, if not longer.

What are the youngest Americans actually like? Caricatured in elite media as Instagram-addicted dilettantes crashing multiple industries with their bizarre tastes and proclivities, and consumed with unearned self-regard, the youngest Americans are, instead, incredibly resilient and delightful people, forced to confront a runaway planetary disaster produced by their parents and grandparents and facing uncertain economic and political futures. Chapter 4 offers a demographic profile of millennials and Generation Z, which will help explain why young people have been voting Democratic for so long. It will also explore why people in certain demographic groups (like African Americans and Latinx) tend to vote so heavily Democratic, connecting the dots between the more diverse younger generations and the voting patterns that are becoming more and more apparent.

But of course, not *all* the kids are left. If you've spent any time watching Fox News lately, you could be forgiven for thinking the network's gaggle of aggressive young conservatives probably represents the country's future. They don't, but that doesn't mean that they shouldn't be dismissed as a force in American politics. Chapter 5 will look at some of the leaders and organizations of the new right, from the chapters of the campus agitprop shop Turning Points USA to the writing of pundits like Ben Shapiro and Tomi Lahren. But it will also highlight some polling data that should confound typical expectations. While the bomb-throwing young media personalities represent a kind of hyperaggressive partisanship and an in-your-face culture war aesthetic, the numbers currently on young Republicans suggests that the media warriors are outliers and that young Republicans are more liberal, especially on social issues, than older Republicans.

Chapter 6 ties it all together in a neat little bow for those of you too lazy to read the whole thing. The conclusion will think about what an American political world dominated by an ever-expanding demographic cohort of left-leaning voters would look and feel like and argues that we may be living through the first stages of one of the country's periodic realignments, when the basic coalitions that undergird each party's power shift just enough to produce a new and lasting landscape of competition. It looks at some of the ways Democrats might blow it, including not moving aggressively enough to reform the country's political institutions, protecting the power and privilege of party elites at the expense of younger and hungrier activists, and failing to plan for and protect against the political fallout of some of the most ambitious plans of the progressive left. Finally, it entertains some darker scenarios concerning how our friends across the aisle might react as their political power, cultural influence, and misbegotten capitalist dystopia slowly—and then perhaps suddenly—slips away from them. Can the United States hold together under this kind of strain? Are the country's institutions strong enough to withstand the orgy of whining, rule-bending, violence-threatening, and violence-doing that Republicans are going to cling to on their way out of power?

I can sense that you're starting to worry that you might be holding some kind of dreary data dump in your hands. I would like to assure you: there aren't that many statistics in this book! The professor who taught me quantitative analysis in graduate school would be happy to tell you that I have no business writing that kind of book anyway. There is some survey data here and there, some election results and polling crosstabs. But the truth is that it really isn't super complicated or hard to see what is happening here, both because these numbers are extremely stark and impossible to interpret any other way and also because you can see with your own two eyes what is happening in this country and how young people feel about it. The aggrieved, sniveling, emotionally incontinent, elderly white racists who were put in charge of the United States in 2016 are truly doing everything in their power to ensure they are despised by supermajorities of everyone under the age of forty. The whole spectacle has been so relentlessly repellent that the kids are disproportionately vibing on a septuagenarian socialist named Bernie Sanders, a guy who would have been so far out of the American mainstream two decades ago that he would have needed a GPS just to find his way back to the center.[13]

The bad news is that these imbeciles, grifters, and cryptofascists still might win the 2020 elections, for a variety of dispiriting and infuriating reasons discussed later in this book. Telling you that young voters lean heavily left and that they will never change is not to tell you that any of this is going to be easy.

But the good news is that, whatever happens in 2020, young voters are poised to deliver victory after victory to Democrats nationwide, to break open the US political system, finally allowing for the kind of bold, progressive legislation people on the left have been dreaming about for a generation.

CHAPTER I

POLAR OPPOSITES

I DON'T KNOW about you, but if you're roughly my age (forty-two, when this thing goes to press), the political world of your adult life feels quite different than the one you were introduced to as a teenager, kind of like downsizing from a single-family house to a room in a highway-side, strip-mall motel. The first time I voted, in 1994, politics felt like a contest between two basically normal parties, who differed on where tax rates should be set and the details of abortion laws and how much money should be spent on defense. But at the presidential level, they didn't seem that far apart—at least, not so distant from each other that losing an election would feel like an existential crisis. For people my age and older, this has probably been the most difficult fact about American politics to accept—that elections are no longer like baseball games, where sharp-elbowed competition between the teams on the field ends with sportsmanlike hand-shaking and intonations of "good game" when the contest is over. Rather, they are more like wars, where the losing side must immediately confront the scale of damage to its vital interests and contemplate the bleak postsurrender future. This is not to say that elections in the 1970s and 1980s didn't have stakes—they certainly did. A lot of the political science nostalgia for the bipartisanship of the 1950s and 1960s glosses over how much of it was dedicated to a pact between the parties to prevent progress on civil rights and to avoid a reckoning with America's founding sins. And the period saw its fair share of nasty episodes as well as the first inklings of the new, hardball style of politics that would characterize the twenty-first century. But few would say they truly feared democracy itself was at stake in those elections.

In 1988, the first election I have any clear memory of, Democratic candidate Michael Dukakis ran on a platform of leveraging public-private partnerships to rebuild distressed areas of the country. He talked about cutting specific defense programs, like Reagan's Star Wars boondoggle, but refused to commit to an overall reduction in the military budget.[1] Both he and Republican nominee George H. W. Bush were in favor of free-trade agreements with other countries. While most people remember only the awful moment in which Dukakis was asked whether he would favor the death penalty if his wife Kitty was raped and murdered, the debates between the two men were relatively staid affairs.[2] When Dukakis was finished with his now-infamous answer to the question, Bush reiterated his support for the death penalty and said, "And so we just have an honest difference of opinion. I support it and he doesn't."[3] When the topic of abortion came up, Bush stated, "It is personal," and, looking at Dukakis, said, "and I don't assail him on that issue or others on that issue." While the general contours of disagreement between the two parties would seem somewhat familiar to viewers today, the differences between Bush and Dukakis were clearly less substantively sharp than what characterizes the two parties today. Moreover, it was also evident that the two men did not have complete contempt for each other in the same way that Barack Obama and Mitt Romney did in 2012 or Donald Trump and Hillary Clinton in 2016. (The story of American politics in my lifetime can, in some ways, be encapsulated by deteriorating body language of the candidates at these debates.)

I don't remember particularly widespread devastation in my household when Dukakis lost that election to Bush. There were no scenes like those of emotionally ruined Clinton supporters in 2016, weeping into one another's shoulders like the *Challenger* had just exploded with their dog on it. Maybe that's because the outcome was a foregone conclusion and the election wasn't terribly close. But that was the case in 2012 too, and it didn't stop Romney boosters from having messy breakdowns on live television. And particularly for those who leave it all on the field for these campaigns, crashing on couches, knocking on doors until their feet go numb and their voices hoarse, making call after call to hostile strangers in makeshift campaign offices, it makes sense that they would lose it if it all slips away, in the same way that players from the losing team in the World Series often perch themselves on the dugout rail and wipe away hot tears as they watch their opponents dogpile and pop champagne as the cameras trail them around. But it feels like the raw emotions of campaign staffers and candidates have now been transferred, en masse, to the rest of us.

On election night in 2016, I thought about the damage Trump's policy proposals, including eliminating protections for preexisting conditions, could do to my own family. Just four months earlier, my wife had donated a kidney to my mother-in-law, an incredible gift and also a draining ordeal. We watched the horrifying Republican National Convention while she recovered at her aunt and uncle's house in Maryland. Years shy of eligibility for Medicare, it was unclear what would happen to my mother-in-law if the protections of Obamacare were torched by Congressional Republicans in a fit of resentment against President Obama. I had undocumented students who were now in real danger of getting deported to countries they had not visited since they were small children. The Iranian American family I married into faced an uncertain future in terms of visiting their homeland or relatives who lived in Europe, and the promise of the 2015 Iran Deal was likely to be destroyed. More so than in any election in my lifetime, 2016 felt personal, like the outcome had the potential not just to result in national policy calamity, as was entirely predictable on election night in 2000, but to ruin me personally and directly. I thrummed with both rage and despair. The bitterness I felt for the millions of people who had voted for this awful, joyless sociopath was all-consuming. My feelings about the ninety-one million eligible voters who sat out the election are best not repeated here.

What the hell happened to me? In early September of that year, I had assigned a chapter from a Matthew Flinders' *Defending Politics: Why Democracy Matters in the Twenty-First Century* to my students in an introductory American politics seminar. I was determined to convince them that there was more to politics than naked cynicism, that most people who sought elected office were decent people who wanted to gain power so they could achieve their vision of the greater good, that democracy is never perfect, that it is in some ways less efficient and satisfying than authoritarianism, and that the policy solutions it delivers frequently satisfy no one, especially the most ideologically committed. Or as Flinders puts it, "In the absence of any broad public understanding of the simple aims, limits and costs of democracy, modern politics will inevitably contain the seeds of its own ruin because at the root of democratic politics lies a set of hard truths, which we ignore at our peril."[4] I wanted students to see those limitations without losing the understanding that democracy is the only way to settle our differences without killing one another.

That early semester optimist was difficult to square with the hollowed-out, dispirited professor who had to roll in to teach class the day after the election. I had promised the class that I would eat my suit jacket if Trump won Pennsylvania, only to inform them that on my salary, I simply could not afford to dine on my one good sports coat. Twenty years ago, I had hobnobbed happily with campus Republicans the night Bill Clinton beat out Bob Dole and Ross Perot to win a second term. As a young staffer at the long-gone World Almanac and Book of Facts, I had followed along the postelection drama in 2000 between Bush and Gore with fascination and occasional frustration but rarely despair. I loved politics. But on that day in 2016, I honestly wasn't even sure I wanted to teach or study it anymore. I wondered how I would deal with the students who had voted for Trump—not that we would argue or that I would give them bad grades or be mean to them, but how would I integrate their views into a classroom? My partisanship, which I worked hard, although probably not especially successfully, to hide, felt like it had shape-shifted. Was this really about policy differences anymore? Do democracies not have the right to diminish the scale of the benefits they offer citizens or create new laws to govern who may enter the country, how long they may stay, and whether they can become citizens? Had Jeb Bush run on roughly the same platform as Donald Trump, would I have been so crushed?

The answer to that question lies in the hallowed fields of political science, where scholars have spent decades asking difficult questions like the ones I was wrestling with as I faced my mostly hopeless students that day. And the consensus in the scholarly community is that yes, both Americans individually and our elected officials in Congress are more divided than they have been in more than a century. In 2014, media outlets reported some extremely disturbing study results. Americans not only expressed increasingly negative evaluations of members of the opposite political party, but for the first time, significant numbers of people extended those evaluations into the personal sphere. Some 49 percent of Republicans said they would be "displeased" if their kids married a Democrat, and 33 percent of Democrats said the same about Republicans.[5] The new *Guess Who's Coming to Dinner* wasn't your kid bringing home someone of a different race, but rather an intern for *The Federalist or Current Affairs*. Dropping a Republican into a family Christmas party of Democrats promises to ruin everyone's fun, and family relations can be tense and difficult to navigate as it is without dragging politics into it. We're generally only one ill-considered comment away from red-faced shouting, finger-pointing and hard feelings, usually as the less committed partisans in the family look on in horror or stare down while moving the potatoes around on their plate aimlessly. Many of us now profess to enjoy drinking one another's tears.

During the Obama era, scholars started to turn their attention to what they called *polarization*—the way voters and politicians seemed to be growing further apart in their policy proposals and governing philosophies and even their attitudes. I want to take a moment to highlight a particularly important distinction that often gets lost in these kinds of discussions. Polarization is not a synonym for "closely or evenly divided." In other words, it is possible for American elections to be achingly close year after year without either the electorate or the politicians themselves being characterized as polarized. Countries, like the United States today, where power changes hands between political parties very frequently should be thought of as having "high volatility." It is an easier concept to graft onto European parliamentary democracies that feature multiple competitive parties arrayed on a left–right ideological spectrum. In these countries, you would describe the system as increasingly polarized the further apart the most extreme left and right parties are from one another in terms of their platforms, ideologies, policies and goals. So when we say that American politics are polarized, we do not necessarily mean that elections will automatically be close. We mean that Democrats and Republicans are further apart ideologically than at any time in recent memory.

How do we know this is true? Intrepid researchers have spent decades studying ideology in both chambers of Congress. At UCLA, political scientists have used roll call votes in Congress to estimate an ideological score for each member of the House and Senate going back to 1880. On this scale, −1 is perfectly liberal, and +1 is perfectly conservative.[6] The scores of all members can then be averaged to create a party mean for each caucus in any given Congress. This data is by

POLAR OPPOSITES ★ 39

no means perfect and carries with it some of the researchers' assumptions about what constitutes left and right on a variety of issues. It also assumes that roll call votes in the House and Senate are a perfect proxy for someone's ideology, which is obviously not the case at the more granular level. But it's the best information currently available and is the only way to measure ideological polarization going back to the distant past. And what they have found is that the difference between the ideological center of gravity in each party has never been larger.

For example: In the 115th Congress, Republican Senator Dean Heller represented the ideological center of his party, with twenty-seven Republicans less and twenty-seven more conservative. In the 91st Congress (1969–71), there were only five Republican senators with a more conservative voting record than Heller, among them the party's 1964 presidential candidate, Arizona Senator Barry Goldwater. In that Congress, there were Republicans who were more liberal than other Democrats, and vice versa. To no surprise, the most liberal Republicans were from the Northeast—New Jersey, New York, and Massachusetts, states that would become ironclad Democratic strongholds in the decades to come. Likewise, many Democrats who were more conservative than some liberal Republicans were from the soon-to-be-lost Deep South, like James Eastland of Mississippi. Eastland, who made an infamous cameo in the 2020 Democratic primary after dying thirty-four years prior when former Vice President Joe Biden used him—a white supremacist—as an example of the kind of Republican he was able to cut deals with when he joined the Senate in 1973.[7]

There are two ways of visualizing what has happened in American politics since the 1970s. One is to look at the party mean in each chamber over time. In these graphs, upward movement on the y axis represents a shift in a more conservative direction, and downward movement shows a trend toward a more liberal ideology. The charts track these shifts going back to 1880 (on the x axis).

HOUSE

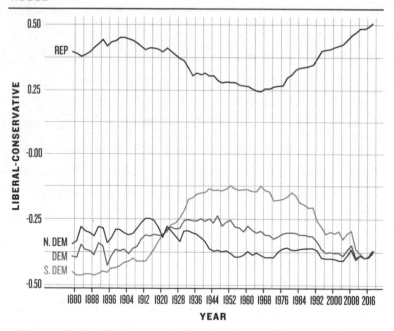

SENATE

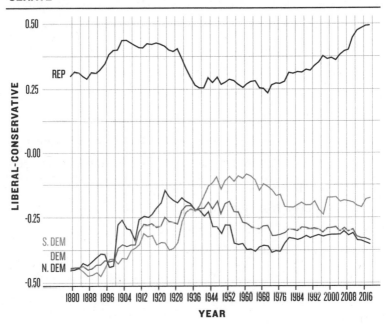

You don't have to be a data scientist to see what's going on here. Beginning in 1970, the Republican Party began a long drift rightward, a process that had three real inflection points: the election of Republican presidents Ronald Reagan in 1980 and George W. Bush in 2000, and then the groundbreaking victory of Democrat Barack Obama in 2008, the first African American president in American history. The sharpest and most sudden movement upward—that is, toward harder-line conservatism—in fact, followed Obama's election, a piece of data that feels quite easy to square with our anecdotal experience of the last twelve years of history. It wasn't just then-Senate Minority Leader Mitch McConnell's much-derided declaration that "the single most important thing we want to achieve is for President Obama to be a one-term president." (McConnell actually said this just before the 2010 midterms and noted that if Obama were "willing to do a Clintonian backflip," Republicans might be willing to work with him.)[8] It was also partly because two Democratic wave elections in 2006 and 2008 had wiped out many moderate Republicans, the GOP was indeed much more hard-right than it had been just a few years earlier.

During this time period, the Republican upward movement toward harder-line conservatism was not nearly matched in scale by a Democratic move toward the bottom of the chart. Political scientists Matt Grossman and David Hopkins described this as "asymmetric polarization"—with a Republican Party increasingly acting like a European-style ideological party and a Democratic Party that remained a collection of interest groups and politicians seeking to satisfy different parts of the party's coalition.[9] Even with the Democratic Party moving leftward since 2010 (again, largely because of the annihilation of the party's moderates in consecutive midterm wipeouts in 2010 and 2014), the Republican Party remains significantly more conservative than the Democratic Party is liberal, leading to things like the odd spectacle of presidential candidates like Joe Biden and Amy Klobuchar promising to find common legislative ground with Republicans, who are almost certain to scorn them should either be elected president.

The other way to look at the data is to think about the quantitative distance between the two parties ideologically. The following chart captures the difference between the two parties' mean ideology scores, averaged from all Republican and Democratic members of the House and Senate going back to 1880. When the lines dip down, it means there is very little difference between the average Republican and the average Democrat. When it spikes upward, it means there are huge ideological divides between Democrats and Republicans in Congress.

LIBERAL-CONSERVATIVE PARTISAN POLARIZATION BY CHAMBER

Two things stand out: since Reagan, the House has always been more polarized than the Senate. Even as recently as 2004, the Senate was a much more ideologically heterodox place. But especially in recent years, the Senate has nearly caught the House. Both chambers have become much more sharply polarized since 1970, with the ideological distance between the parties basically doubling over the course of a generation. In a system whose rules nearly always require some level of bipartisanship to get significant legislation passed, this yawning gap between the two parties has become a more and more serious obstacle to policymaking. The divided governments of the 112th–114th Congresses (2011–2017) were the least productive in terms of the number of laws passed since the end of the Civil War. The 116th Congress, with a Democratic House and a Republican Senate, is currently on track to be even worse at passing laws.[10] The United States might not be a society in total free fall or on the verge of an Easter Island–style collapse, but it is also not a country bereft of serious problems in need of vigorous and creative policy solutions.

For the uninitiated, I'm going to introduce you now to one of the great tropes of comparative political science: the 2 x 2 chart. The chart looks at four possible ways of describing a political system across two variables: polarization and volatility. Polarization, again, is simply a measure of how far apart ideologically two parties (or their supporters) are. Whereas volatility, as you'll recall, is a measure of how frequently power changes hands. In high-volatility countries, major parties have similar levels of popular support and trade places in government quite often. In low-volatility countries, one party or coalition has significantly more public support than its main rivals and therefore finds itself in power more often than not. Ireland provides, what I would argue is, a good example. Modern Ireland, for instance, has been dominated by two similar parties—Fine Gael and Fianna Fáil, which are difficult to distinguish ideologically. In 2016, the two parties combined for more than 50 percent of the total votes for parliament. Despite their overall similarities, the two parties compete sharply for votes and power. In Japan, which is neither polarized nor closely divided, the Liberal-Democratic Party (LDP) has won nearly every national election since World War II. While other parties in the system have wildly different ideologies, they are not serious competitors for power and are thus mostly extraneous. Finally, Germany is polarized—the ideological distance between left-wing Die Linke and the right-wing Alternative For Germany—is vast. Both parties are now strong enough to conceivably be part of a coalition government. Yet the centrist Christian Democratic Union continues to dominate national politics, as it has for more than a decade.

	HIGH VOLATILITY	LOW VOLATILITY
POLARIZED	United States	Germany
NOT POLARIZED	Ireland	Japan

In many multiparty democracies, the smaller, more ideologically extreme parties can score a small number of seats in election after election and be content with it. There may be no real incentives for such parties to moderate their issue stances to appeal to more voters and thus to gain more power in parliament. Hard-left and hard-right parties that would be considered fringe in America routinely score seats in parliamentary democracies. In the Netherlands, for example, one of the seated parties in parliament is called The Party For Animals, a party dedicated to fighting for the welfare and dignity of our nonhuman friends. But in the United States, polarization has tended to be associated with a closely divided electorate because when one party scored multiple substantial election victories in a row, it has generally had the effect of pulling the other party toward it, like a tractor beam. When Democrats dominated American politics from the 1930s to the 1960s, they dragged the center of the Republican Party leftward with them, until a new generation of ideological entrepreneurs, led by Barry Goldwater and Ronald Reagan, captured the party and reoriented its course rightward. Similarly, the ascendance and then dominance of Republicans from the late 1960s to the early 1990s had the same effect on Democrats.

In the US political system in particular, the growth of diametrically opposed beliefs in America's two major parties is a problem if for no other reason than the system design frequently requires intra- and inter-branch cooperation across party lines. Indeed, the Constitution's architects somewhat infamously assumed that there wouldn't be political parties or factions. Political differences, of course, are baked into the very concept of democracy, and political parties are the vehicles for expressing and representing those differences in every democracy on the planet (and even in some non-democracies).

There isn't a single successful, longstanding democratic society anywhere in the world where power is not contested and wielded by political parties. For those parties to have any meaning, they must offer voters real differences in terms of the policy proposals and ideas they back, especially if parties are to serve as a kind of informational shortcut for voters who lack the time and energy to exhaustively research the background of every single candidate running for public office. In fact, political scientists were so convinced that ideological parties were important that a committee of the American Political Science Association issued a report in 1950 called "Toward a More Responsible Two-Party System" that recommended sharper distinctions between Democrats and Republicans.[11] And there is no question that, in many countries, voters have available to them significant political parties that are ideologically much farther apart than Democrats and Republicans were recently. And to a certain extent, that's good. Otherwise, politics might ultimately look to most people like a noisy but inconsequential sport, as two or more groups of elites with indistinguishable views takes turns governing the country in their own interest. That is, not surprisingly, the way many nonvoters feel about American politics, which shocks committed partisans about every four years or so.

Few would dispute the idea that polarization is a problem in American politics, but there is actually substantial disagreement about its shape and causes. On one side are scholars who believe polarization in the electorate is overstated—Americans actually don't disagree about policy as much as they think they do or nearly as much as media elites believe. A plurality of adults, in fact, falls into what one recent survey deemed "the exhausted majority," people who are turned off by rabid partisanship and tend to have down-the-middle views on divisive issues like abortion and climate change. Unfortunately, their views are drowned out by other, smaller, louder groups of Americans, committed to partisan combat and victory at all costs. "These tensions are poisoning personal relationships, consuming our politics and putting our democracy in peril," the authors of "Hidden Tribes" write.[12]

The political scientist Lilliana Mason has perhaps become the best-known advocate of the idea that polarization isn't necessarily based on policy differences but rather on the social psychology of group conflict in human societies. "The primary result of group membership," Mason argues, "is simply to hold positive feelings for the ingroup, and no positive feelings toward outsiders."[13] For Mason, party identification in the United States now more closely reflects this ingroup-out-group social dynamic than it does actual policy differences between the two parties. While "the parties should be distinguishable and unique," Democrats and Republicans have become "socially polarized."[14] Partisans put the interest of their party first. They engage in "motivated reasoning," which is the process of fitting new information into your existing beliefs rather than trying to test those beliefs against the available evidence. Worst of all, this "affective polarization" means that Democrats and Republicans don't want to live near one another, don't want to marry one another, don't want their kids to marry one another, and they hold very negative views of members of the other party. This mutual loathing is completely out of proportion with the real differences between members of the two parties. More disturbingly, it is the most politically engaged citizens who seem most susceptible to this kind of thinking, and the least informed who are open to being persuaded to switch their votes between elections.

Not everyone, however, believes that differences between the parties are more emotional than grounded in policy differences. Alan Abramowitz, in *The Great Alignment*, notes that today's divisions are the result of a long-term reordering of American politics around issue differences rather than emotional tensions. For Abramowitz, what has happened since the 1960s is that voters have increasingly aligned themselves with the party that represents their interests and policy preferences. He writes, "Partisan polarization among political elites cannot be understood unless we take into account the parallel rise in polarization in the public as a whole."[15] Since the 1960s, political behaviors indicative of polarization in the electorate are undeniable. The practice of "split-ticket voting," that is, voting for one party's candidate for one office and a different party's candidate for another office elsewhere on the ballot, is in terminal decline. Higher and higher numbers of self-identified Democrats and Democratic leaners vote for the Democratic Party's presidential candidate, and vice versa, whereas in the past, many more voters would desert their party's standard bearer on election day. Abramowitz acknowledges, of course, the rise of affective polarization, or what he calls "negative partisanship," but locates its causes in the fact that "partisan identities have become increasingly aligned with other social and political divisions."[16]

Election day polling suggests that Abramowitz has a point. Whatever they may tell the Gallup and Pew people when they come calling, on election day Democrats and Republicans express very different views on a host of interrelated issues that generally line up quite well with each party's political-economic philosophy. In the '60s and '70s, for example, many Democrats held racist views on civil rights issues even as the party moved slowly to the forefront of efforts to rectify America's historic sins. Yet today, Democrats, and white Democrats in particular, have a much more unified set of attitudes about race and racism. The same goes for hot-button issues like abortion and gun rights. Heterodoxy on these issues once characterized both parties. Yet in 2018, 76 percent of Democrats told exit pollsters they wanted stricter gun control laws, and 76 percent of Republicans said they didn't.[17] Overall, 59 percent of the heavily Democratic-leaning 2018 electorate wanted stricter laws, and 36 percent opposed such changes. These figures are hard to reconcile with non-election-day polling about these matters. In 2017, Pew polled Americans about this question, and found that 52 percent of Americans wanted stricter gun laws, 30 percent wanted no change, and 18 percent wanted less strict laws. The election day polling allows for much less nuance than an extended Pew or Gallup survey. Where, for instance, do the 43 percent of Republicans who told Pew in 2017 that they wanted stricter background check laws go on election day? They go to the Republican Party. Elections in America, by their nature, convert public opinion that may exist on a broad spectrum into what is, essentially, a binary choice.

Abortion is another illustrative case for these dynamics. For years, Gallup has asked a three-part question: Do you think abortion should be legal under any circumstances, legal only under certain circumstances, or illegal in all circumstances? These numbers have been remarkably stable since 1975, with a clear national consensus for "legal only under certain circumstances," which has fluctuated between 48 and 61 percent of respondents but which has usually been in the low 50s. For such a number to exist in a three-way question in which significant numbers of people choose the two extremes, it must be a consensus that transcends political parties. But on election day 2018, when exit pollsters asked about Roe v. Wade, Democrats wanted to keep it as is 69–21, and Republicans wanted to overturn in 59–30. There are only two choices, and given those two choices, people generally lined up behind the position of their preferred political party. Polarized? Effectively polarized? Until we have a multiparty political system in the United States, we really have no way of knowing for sure, and it's not super clear if it makes much of a difference either way. Voters from the two parties increasingly hate one another, send politicians with wildly different visions of the public good to DC, and then punish heretics come primary season.

For Abramowitz, it is race that has fundamentally altered American politics. As the share of the nonwhite population has grown, through differential birth rates and immigration, conservative white voters have migrated to the Republican Party, which has been incentivized over time to respond to the interests of those voters. Meanwhile, the Democratic Party has become ever more reliant on nonwhite voters. The two parties are now characterized by ideological, racial, and cultural divisions that align neatly with one another. Both Mason and Abramowitz agree that the absence of what scholars call "cross-cutting cleavages" (i.e. a highly educated professor who is also an Evangelical Christian) contributes to polarization by making it easier for people to sort themselves into the "correct" tribe and never have sustained interaction with anyone who disagrees. Individuals are now much more likely to tell pollsters that they agree with the Democratic or Republican position across a range of seemingly unrelated issue positions.

Whatever you ultimately think of this debate, the reality is that this "exhausted majority," inasmuch as it exists, has so far been incapable of translating its desire for bipartisanship, compromise and practical politics into electoral outcomes that incentivize the kind of behavior they tell pollsters they want to see. Even if Mason and the "Hidden Tribes" scholars are correct that polarization is less about policy and more about negative partisanship and emotion, no one has a particularly compelling idea for how to get political elites to change their strategies. Exhausted or not, people keep showing up on election days, electing Democrats and Republicans and then telling pollsters they agree with the issue positions of their party leaders. And whether it is elite-driven or policy-driven, the reality is that there really are two opposing camps in American politics today. Those camps are increasingly hardened and steered by people whose policy views are perhaps somewhat out of step with median public opinion but nevertheless well within the boundaries of normal discourse and "acceptable" views. Any project that seeks to bring people together in spite of these realities is probably going to come to ruin.

Polarization in the context of fairly evenly divided parties has produced governing stasis in the United States because of how often power has shifted between Democrats and Republicans and how far apart our elected officials are ideologically, as we saw in the charts above. You could easily argue that apart from the GOP's tax reform bill in 2017, not a single meaningful piece of legislation has been passed in the United States since 2011. It has also produced a number of very close elections, with the two parties gaining similar numbers of overall votes since the turn of the century. In the House, for instance, Democrats have received 497 million votes since 2000, and Republicans 485 million. In percentage terms, that's about 50.6 percent for Democrats, and 49.4 percent for Republicans—and those numbers are of all votes cast for the two parties in races for the House of Representatives over the last twenty years! As with the Senate and the presidency, under a fairer system, Democrats would have seen much better outcomes during this time period. But there is no question that even if the country overall has leaned slightly left since 2000 (debatable, since many Democratic aggregate vote edges are disproportionately drawn from one blowout presidential election in 2008), the edge is relatively small, and that both Democrats and Republicans can claim with some logic to hold the allegiance of roughly half the country's voters.

To reiterate: these election totals did not have to produce the bitter, combustible paralysis they did. If Democratic and Republican elected officials did not believe diametrically different things about the role of the government in the provision of health care, for instance, it might have been possible to negotiate a sensible set of reforms to mend Obamacare or reform immigration laws. That these compromises are pretty obvious, and that ordinary people always tell pollsters they want politicians to work toward them did nothing to crack the ugly stalemate in DC. And that's because elections weren't just relentlessly close, but because voters were sending people to Washington who had very little to talk about let alone to negotiate.

It is also relatively unobjectionable to say that this is all distinctly unpleasant for America's voters. It is one thing to disagree about some policy issue, and to settle those differences at the ballot box or to engage in sustained activism for change. But tensions are running high. "Close your eyes and imagine holding someone's scalp in your hands," wrote one Federalist scribe as he imagined how Republicans should handle a left-wing future.[18] Musing about a second Civil War has become quite commonplace in certain segments of the right during the Trump administration—and most of it happened when the GOP was in control of both Congress and the presidency. Commentators on the left envision a "Bluexit," which writer Kevin Baker describes as the process of "blue states and cities" choosing "to effectively abandon the American national enterprise, as it is currently constituted."[19]

Scholars and activists have floated various kinds of proposals to combat runaway polarization in the United States. Gerrymandering—the process of drawing district lines to benefit one's own party and disadvantage the other, a practice unique to American democracy—likely contributes to polarization, since it has, over time, helped create more "safe seats" in the House of Representatives, typically occupied by ever-more-radical partisans who only have to answer to their own primary voters. Many scholars propose nonpartisan redistricting commissions of the sort that now exist in some US states and that are being hotly pursued by activists in many others. As the political scientist Elaine Karmack argues, "taking redistricting out of the hands of state legislatures and placing it in the hands of non-partisan commissions is an obvious place to start to reduce polarization."[20] Enthusiasts of redistricting reform also frequently cite campaign finance reform as a mechanism for reducing polarization, although in a post–Citizens United world, it is not clear how any such mechanisms will survive legal challenge, at least until the current Supreme Court majority is flipped.

Others blame the parties themselves, including America's primary elections. The United States is, indeed, an outlier in how deeply voters are involved in choosing the general election candidates of Republicans and Democrats. Because primary elections are generally low-turnout affairs and because it is largely the most committed partisans in each party who show up, primaries may have the effect of skewing representation toward the extremes even though the vast majority of voters—who ignore primary elections—would prefer other types of candidates. Some, including the eminent political scientist Arend Lijphart, suggest abolishing primaries altogether, since "primaries are clearly not a necessary ingredient of democracy."[21] Others, recognizing how that might be viewed by voters, suggest reinstituting greater party control over the primary process. As Nathaniel Persily argues, "the party organization could own the brand and decide which candidates get to use it."[22] That might have prevented the rise of Donald Trump as a hostile force in the Republican Party; however, it is not clear what greater party control would do to reduce polarization in the context of a GOP that has been thoroughly conquered by Trumpism. The truth is that whatever the merits of the American primary system, going back to an era of greater party control over these elections is fanciful. It flies directly in the face of voter expectations about how these elections should be structured and run.

Scholars of comparative politics believe that "ranked choice voting" could contribute to a decrease in this sharp polarization, by shifting the incentives for candidates who currently have no need to craft a message that appeals beyond their own narrow bases. Instead of voting for a single candidate as we do in most elections in the United States, voters would be able to rank-order the candidates on the ballot. The nonpartisan reform organization Fair Vote has, for years, been pushing a proposal that would create larger congressional districts of three to five people elected using this procedure, an idea that I am on record fully supporting.[23] And while ranked choice voting is definitely catching on—it is how Maine now elects its members of the House and was recently passed into law by voters in New York City—we are years away from this system transforming national politics. Others trot out familiar ideas like legislative term limits—a favorite of concrete-skinned old billionaire Tom Steyer, who made this zombie idea one of the centerpieces of his wasteful campaign for the Democratic nomination last year.

Most people are long on explanations of polarization and pretty short on ideas about how to fix it without major reforms of the political system itself. The authors of "Hidden Tribes" conclude their report with some suggestions about how to address bare-knuckle political combat. One idea: "Political candidates can speak to the values that unify the nation with a larger 'we,' instead of mobilizing their base while polarizing the country." Another proposal: "Technology companies can turn their vast resources and analytical tools to creating platforms and systems that help do the hard work of bringing people together, rather than the easy work of magnifying outrage in echo chambers and filter bubbles."[24] This would be great, of course, but there are two problems with this kind of wishful thinking. First, we *had* a political leader who spent eight years speaking about "we" and, despite occasional missteps, remained relentlessly committed to positive rhetoric and was committed to reaching across the aisle long after it became apparent that his counterparts would never do anything but swat his hand away. Americans, indeed, responded to the presidency of Barack Obama by becoming even more polarized, by seeking comfort in bizarre conspiracy theories and enriching and expanding the power of partisan media organizations like *Fox News* and *Breitbart*.

The emergence of politicians who "can speak to the values that unify the nation," in the words of the "Hidden Tribes" report, moreover, is likely to be the result of decreased polarization, rather than its cause. Candidates who position themselves in the moderate middle haven't had much luck at all recently in Democratic and Republican presidential primaries. And tech companies are unlikely to revise their business models for the sake of the public good. If anything, like Facebook, they will make a show of their civic-mindedness only to, in the end, choose whatever path promises the most cash to the largest number of investors. "Doing the hard work of bringing people together" sucks as a business model, and the tech companies won't change unless we force them to. Moreover, simpleminded solutions which look at polarization only from one angle—as the product of electoral institutions, or the physical separation of differently minded Americans, or the filter bubbles produced by social media, or the unseemly rhetoric of political leaders themselves, or our own civic failings, or the inadequacy of civic education in high schools and colleges or false consciousness, or whatever, are inevitably going to run into the difficult reality that our awful politics are produced by all of these factors working in tandem, a self-reinforcing dynamic that is difficult to approach from the perspective of wonky public policy. After all, if bold policy is required to break the polarized stalemate, and the polarized stalemate rarely produces even bare electoral majorities and the underlying institutions make that change even harder, then where are we?

Mason's well-intended ideas don't seem much more realistic. She suggests sending "Democrats and Republicans into the same social arenas and ask them to simply see each other with a calm and friendly set of eyes."[25] This is best achieved by media organizations themselves exposing their viewers and readers to different perspectives, but Mason admits this is unlikely under present circumstances. She yearns for party leaders to "stand up for norms of civil partisan interaction" and discards this idea too. Finally, she notes that "if, however, the status or coherence of the Republican Party declines in the next few years or decades, it may be the case that increasing numbers of Republicans will choose to exit the group (likely becoming independents)."[26] In more simpler terms: if the Republican Party starts losing elections decisively, people might start leaving it, or else dedicate themselves to rescuing the GOP from the dying white racists currently at its core.

Here we arrive at the reality. There are no technocratic solutions to polarization. No number of ice cream socials or media reforms or institutional design gimmicks is going to change the unfortunate mess in American politics today. Some of these ideas are things I believe in fervently, and I do think they could help around the margins. But just getting them passed nationally requires a victory on a scale that is difficult to envision based on recent history. Partisan differences are deeply ingrained, reinforced by social media, demography and choice and sticky enough to persist throughout whole lifetimes. That's the bad news. The predicament is likely to get more dire and uglier before it becomes better. The good news is that one of the two camps is getting smaller, retreating to its sturdiest redoubts in the South and the sparsely inhabited Mountain West and plains states and increasingly reliant on the votes of people who are aging and dying and the archaic quirks of America's rickety political order. Instead of figuring out how to bring these increasingly radicalized people to some kind of gigantic truth-and-reconciliation dinner, the truth is that we really just need to wait for them to die and be replaced.

Polarization will not end because we want it to. It will end when one side wins a series of decisive national victories, forces people to evacuate from the losing party and convinces those who remain to change that party's trajectory. As noted earlier, partisans on both sides have repeatedly and falsely convinced themselves that victories in elections this century would usher in a long period of dominance in national politics, only to discover that the dead don't die. This inability of either Democrats or Republicans to press their advantage for extended periods of time is partly the result of US political institutions, which force Americans to issue a verdict on party performance just two years into a presidential term, an absurdly short calendar that simply does not allow the public to truly evaluate the results of policies. But it is also the result of a fairly evenly divided—that is, volatile—electorate. But it does not look like that division will last much longer.

In most democratic societies, power is hotly contested, and changes hands with enough frequency that most political actors can convince themselves there is nothing wrong with their message or philosophy or tactics, or that, at worst, those factors need some mild adjustment to win next time around. But it is also not as rare as we might think for one political faction, once competitive if not predominant, to collapse entirely, ushering in a long period of single-party rule. Israel, for example, has not elected a left or even a center-left government since 1999. The Labor Party, which governed the country from its founding in 1948 to the election of Menachem Begin's government in 1977 and which enjoyed multiple stints in power in the 1990s, has been reduced to 5 out of 120 seats in Israel's legislature, the Knesset, in the most recent election. It might as well no longer exist. It's a complex story, involving the failure of the Oslo peace process in the 1990s, the rise of religious radicalism, and the influence of parties in favor of annexing the disputed West Bank and Gaza Strip. But it's also kind of simple—people stopped voting for Labor because the party's policies and its recent record of governance no longer appealed to enough people to make it electorally relevant.

In fact, party *continuity*, a measure of how frequently political parties change names or merge or vanish altogether between elections, is much lower in some other democracies than it is in the United States, where Democrats and Republicans have dominated state and local elections for 150 years. But just because a major American political party has not disappeared since the 1850s does not actually mean that it couldn't happen again. Like all deaths, the demise of a political party is rarely pretty and frequently cruel, and just thinking about it inspires all manner of dread. But Republicans would do well to start contemplating their own political mortality, if for no other reason than to start considering who or what will inherit the low-tax, small-government political philosophy that will continue to have resonance as long as there are elections in the United States.

Because the kids are coming. And they will likely take both of America's political problems—polarization and a closely divided electorate, with them. Today's repellent, radical Republicans should start writing a will, or change.

CHAPTER 2

THE REPUBLICAN YOUTH APOCALYPSE

I THINK YOU probably have a vague sense that young people are not super into the Republican Party. The purpose of this chapter is to convince you that, however bad you think things are between young voters and the GOP today, the reality is much, much worse. Young people are voting Democratic at a scale and duration that is totally unprecedented in the modern polling era. And the truth is that we need them to keep doing this. Because frankly, we're all in a lot of trouble.

One of the great film and television tropes that refuses to die is the protagonist getting into such a terrible fix that he or she is about to be murdered at the hands of the antagonist. Perhaps the killer has the hero pinned to the ground with a knife raised theatrically in the air. Or a gun pointed and ready to finish the job before pausing for a few convenient minutes of exposition. And then the hero's friend or colleague or lover bursts into the room and takes down the villain at the last possible moment. You can think of American democracy, and really the future of human civilization, as on the verge of brutal execution by a particularly bloodthirsty antagonist: the Republican Party of the United States of America, an organization that has, in a few short decades, transformed itself into perhaps the paramount threat to the future of all human life on Earth as well as devolved into an illiberal hotbed of racialized authoritarianism. It has long been full of people who are profoundly hostile to the very idea of democratic majorities coming to power and making law, but in recent years has been taken over by people willing to openly violate core American democratic principles to stay in office. The GOP is pointing a gun at us and explaining why it's about to kill us. And young people, hopefully, will burst through the door to save us just in the nick of time.

The warming of the Earth's climate, driven almost entirely by actions taken during the course of a single human lifetime, threatens to unleash a century of hellish atmospheric change, resource conflict, and runaway suffering, as coastal cities flood, large swathes of the planet become borderline or literally uninhabitable, and longstanding ecosystems are threatened with negative transformation or obliteration. Trillions of dollars in economic damage are virtually ensured—if the planet reaches 3.7 degrees of warming, the losses would exceed $551 trillion, more than twice the total amount of wealth that exists in the world today.[1] And considering that the collapse of small, strategically marginal Syria in 2011 precipitated a refugee crisis which upended the politics of continental Europe for a decade, we can presume that any large-scale forced migration precipitated by climate change or sudden climate disaster could lead to similar upheavals on a much grander scale.

There are so many obstacles to tackling this problem, including, most importantly, the structure of the international political system, whose anarchic nature makes long-term cooperation challenging even under the most auspicious circumstances. The cold incentives of domestic political actors in democracies across the world are also still terribly skewed toward making the safest choices to ensure reelection, none of which at the moment generally involve asking their constituents to make massive changes to their daily lives in the service of preserving the planet for future generations. But the US Republican Party of the twenty-first century is by far the most important obstacle to a sustained global effort to prevent the nightmare scenarios from coming into being.

Since the rise of the Gingrich Republicans in the early '90s, a fragile bipartisan consensus that global warming exists and is a problem has been eclipsed by the GOP's descent into an increasingly paranoid and fragile denialism. During his campaign for the presidency in 1988, George H. W. Bush remarked, "Those who think we are powerless to do anything about the greenhouse effect forget about the 'White House effect.'" Late in his term, he signed on to a plan to create a United Nations Framework Convention on Climate Change, noting "I invite my colleagues from the industrialized world to join in a prompt start on the convention's implementation."[2] Today, the president of the United States proudly proclaims that climate change is "a Chinese hoax[3]" and, after pulling the United States out of the utterly inadequate Paris Climate Accords, remarked that "I believe that there's a change in weather, and I think it changes both ways."[4] His rhetoric is now completely in step with that of the institutional party itself, which has recommitted itself to the human suicide of fossil fuels and is so bent on murdering everyone's grandchildren that the party acquiesced completely to the president's plan to roll back auto emissions standards that even most car manufacturers were willing and able to work toward.

Not content merely with ensuring their descendants will scramble for survival in a wetter, warmer, more chaotic world, Republicans seem intent on destroying American democracy on their way out the door. Having precipitated a decade-long decline in the US's ranking in the august Freedom House democracy scores, the GOP under Trump has accelerated the country's descent into soft authoritarianism, with the president himself nakedly enriching himself at the expense of the public, colluding with hostile foreign powers to undermine US elections, bending the Department of Justice to his ill will and manipulating the decennial census to benefit his Republican allies. Congressional Republicans, who could depose this frighteningly unhinged and dangerous man at any moment and hand the presidency to the fundamentalist, free-market zealot Mike Pence, have passed up every single opportunity they have been afforded even to marginally push back on any of it. Their capitulation is total.

The multifront assault on democracy, though, is hardly limited to President Trump and will surely continue after he is shown the door in 2020 or 2024. Republican legislatures in states like Wisconsin, Michigan, and North Carolina changed laws to neuter incoming Democratic governors; in Georgia, Ohio, and other GOP-run states, voters are purged from the rosters if they go too long without voting—a cynical attempt to drive down turnout among the kind of marginalized people who tend to lean Democratic. In Florida, voters overwhelmingly passed a state constitutional amendment in 2018 restoring the voting rights of formerly incarcerated citizens, only to see the Republican legislature in cahoots with new GOP Governor Ron DeSantis, counterfeit the law by forcing individuals to pay massive legal costs before getting their franchise back. State Republicans have also, of course, been at the forefront of pushing bogus voter ID laws that drive down minority turnout and clamping down on opportunities to vote on campuses, a rather transparent effort to reduce the number of young people able to exercise their right to vote.

A country in which a heavily white minority manipulates elections, consolidates power over the judiciary, deliberately prevents eligible citizens from exercising their right to participate in the process, and watches as outgoing governments change laws and rules to prohibit incoming elected officials from governing is not one that can be described as fully democratic. And these maneuvers, at heart, stem from a justifiable fear of the electorate, of what might transpire if everyone who wanted to vote was able to do so, and how our politics might work if the most indefensible features of the US political order, including the Electoral College, were gone. There is already a nationwide center-left majority, ready to govern if only the institutions would faithfully translate voter sentiment into election outcomes. Republicans know this. It's why they do what they do. To compound these fear and greed-driven assaults on democracy, Republicans face a demographic apocalypse which threatens to consign the GOP to permanent minority status for several generations.

Republican power in the twenty-first century has been heavily dependent on the devotion and turnout of older, white Americans. The three times that support has collapsed or dipped, Democrats won in overwhelming landslides. In terms of raw votes and percentages, the Republican Party has not once this century scored the kind of victory that Democrats have three times now: in 2006, 2008, and 2018. Republican midterm sweeps in 2010 and 2014 were based on comparatively small victories in the aggregate House vote. The one time this century the GOP presidential candidate won the national popular vote, he did so by 2.4 percentage points and just over three million votes, about the same margins by which Hillary Clinton defeated Donald Trump in 2016. America's archaic institutions have now subjected the country to two presidential elections won by the popular vote loser and multiple versions of the Senate where the majority party got its ass kicked five minutes prior but held on to power due to the suboptimal distribution of Democratic voters in various American states. The

GOP's advantage with older voters is well known. But the scale of the party's problems with young voters remains relatively sparsely discussed and studied. And the few scholars and writers who have noticed the phenomenon have generally failed to appreciate the importance of what has already transpired this century in terms of the voting patterns of young Americans.

Think of the GOP as a cruise liner in the Atlantic. The captain spots an iceberg in the distance. The iceberg is youth voting patterns. With each election young people continue voting Democratic in spectacular numbers, that iceberg grows larger. So while the impact is (barely) survivable over one, two, three, or even at this point, nine electoral cycles, if the iceberg keeps growing it will not be survivable any longer. In the voting-eligible population (VEP), it's not like the young voters have cracked off the iceberg and fallen away— they are getting closer to the core. The iceberg contains formations that are now two decades old, like elder millennials who own houses and businesses and have four kids, most of whom are still voting the way they did the day the Iraq War was launched. With each cycle, the iceberg also swells with an incoming cohort of young voters hostile to the Republican Party. I really can't emphasize this point enough: the American voting population now has roughly a twenty-five-year-long cohort of people who vote decisively left. It began with millennials born in 1981 and has continued into the thirteen-year-olds that were surveyed in the last year or so—people born between 2005 and 2006. Some data from the mock K–12 election held prior to the 2016 presidential contest extends that number to 2011, the age of some of the kindergartners who voted in the poll. That cohort is poised to gradually replace the long conservative generation born between 1928 and 1964. The front end of the Silent Generation is ninety-two years old and dying quickly. The tail end is Joe Biden's age and also passing away rapidly.

Republicans are losing the race for young voters and losing it badly. One way to look at this is to ask about party identification, usually referred to in shorthand as "party ID." Pollsters have been asking citizens which party they identify with since the inauguration of the American National Election Study in 1948. Scholars believe that party ID is a helpful way of measuring how voters think of themselves, how they form attachments to political parties and how unfolding political developments and long-term changes in American politics are reflected in the self-identities of individual Americans. As Donald Green, Bradley Palmquist, and Eric Schickler explain in *Partisan Hearts and Minds: Political Parties and the Social Identities of Voters*, "the outstanding characteristic of party identification is its resemblance to other familiar forms of social identification."[5] In other words, party ID is much like other forms of group identity, including religion or social class. It is an attachment that can survive tumultuous political times or even the falling out between a voter and a particular politician. For example, self-identified Republicans may have disapproved of President Bush in 2007 without surrendering their sense of themselves as a member or supporter of the Republican Party. That includes the possibility that this same voter pulled the lever for Barack Obama in 2008 and yet still thought of his or herself as a Republican. However, one of the distinctive trends of the post–Cold War period in American politics is that self-identified Democrats and Republicans have been voting for the nominee of their party at rates that vastly exceed those of the 1950s, 1960s, and 1970s. So while these numbers do jump around a bit, especially in today's polarized context, they do tell us a bit about expected voting patterns. And because party ID is "sticky"—once a voter calls themselves a Democrat, they are unlikely ever to truly give up the label—we can learn a lot about the future shape of American politics by asking about the loyalties of the youngest voters.

How many people in each age demographic express loyalty to the Democratic or Republican parties? Looking at the overall split between Democrats and Republicans in the general population according to Pew, you can see that Democrats have had a party ID advantage throughout the century, with the exception of 2002, when the parties were even. Obviously, that advantage has not always translated into electoral success, which is not surprising since Republicans have generally outperformed their party ID numbers in the post-WWII period. But the general movement in these numbers tracks pretty clearly with overall political developments. In the post-9/11 period, when President George W. Bush was at the height of his popularity, Republicans significantly eroded the Democrats' party ID advantage, and when public opinion began to turn against the Bush administration in 2005, party ID followed suit. Democrats then opened up a huge advantage in the 2006–2009 period, which collapsed back to a small advantage in 2010, when Republicans seized the House of Representatives, and Democratic President Barack Obama was at the nadir of his popularity. And the Democrats' advantage on this measure has been ticking up again since the victory of Donald Trump in the 2016 presidential election, with a huge assist from the president's nonstop barrage of divisive rhetoric, unpopular policies, and unseemly emotional meltdowns. It turns out that having a toxic, impulse-driven, racist mess at the helm of the party is not helpful for its overall image with the electorate.

According to Pew, in 2004, millennials (which Pew defines as those born between 1981 and 1996) said they were Democrats or Democratic-leaners by a 53–38 margin. That gap had grown to 58–34 by 2017, which again is quite unusual, since a Democrat was in power for a significant chunk of this time frame. Millennials have been more Democratic-leaning than the general population by double digits since 2007, in a way that seems genuinely impervious to even the most negative political climate for Democrats. They became even more Democratic than the general population in the run-up to the 2010 midterm elections, which were a decade-altering catastrophe for the Democratic Party. And while the Democrats' advantage with millennials did narrow a bit in the 2013–14 period during which President Obama was again quite unpopular, it never collapsed. And tellingly, the Democratic Party ID advantage with this group rebounded spectacularly in 2015 long before it did with the general public beginning in 2017. The chart below uses Pew's "leaned Party ID" to compare millennials against the overall population. So in 2004, when millennials identified as Democrat or Lean Democrat by a 15-point margin, the country as a whole was only three points more Democratic than Republican. That meant the millennial "swing" toward the Democratic Party was 12 points.

	D	R	OVERALL	SWING
2004	53	38	D +3	+12
2005	55	37	D +7	+11
2006	52	37	D +8	+7
2007	56	35	D +11	+10
2008	61	30	D +12	+19
2009	57	35	D +11	+11
2010	55	36	D +3	+16
2011	53	38	D +5	+10
2012	55	36	D +4	+15
2013	53	37	D +5	+11
2014	53	37	D +5	+11
2015	55	35	D +3	+17
2016	57	35	D +4	+18
2017	58	34	D +8	+16

It is also worth noting that the group under study by Pew here has become larger and more electorally consequential with time. When we look at demographic data election by election, we tend to look at the top-line data about, say, eighteen-to-twenty-nine-year-olds. But the millennial and Generation Z (born 1997 and after) share of the voting-eligible population increasing quickly. In 2000, for instance, millennials were just 4 percent of the VEP. In 2020, they will be 27 percent, with the baby boomer share in steady, if slow, decline.[6] Generation Z will have gone from 4 percent in 2016 to 10 percent in 2020. Mind you—these aren't the predicted shares of the turnout numbers, and because older Americans continue to vote in larger numbers than younger Americans, the political impact of millennials will lag behind their share of the electorate for the foreseeable future. But they do reflect a rapidly changing electorate. If the youngest Americans were tilting Republican in numbers sufficient to begin offsetting the Democrats' advantage with millennials, this wouldn't be so consequential. But they aren't. Pew's comprehensive Generation Z survey has President Trump's approval rating at 30 percent (as opposed to 29 percent with millennials).[7] Seventy percent say they think government should do more to solve problems (as opposed to 64 percent of millennials), and 54 percent believe that humans are causing climate change (compared to 56 percent of millennials). In other words, the data suggests that Generation Z is nearly identical to the millennial generation.

That really should terrify the Republican Party, because the GOP today is so repellent to young voters that they are upending one of the great laws of postwar American politics. As Dan Hopkins of *Five Thirty Eight* noted, "If the president in power is presiding over good times, young voters swing toward that party." However, this does not at all appear to be the case with the Trump presidency. Despite generational lows in unemployment rates, a booming stock market, and even some evidence of middle-class wage growth, young voters have not swung back toward the Republican Party. The uniquely problematic nature of the Trump presidency has therefore transcended its economic record and extended the Democratic Party's long winning streak with incoming eighteen-year-old voters for at least another four years. The Trump administration's inept and dangerous mishandling of the horrifying COVID-19 crisis, which was unfolding as this book went to press, makes it even less likely that Republicans will win over young people anytime soon.

If you stopped looking into it in 2016, you could probably make the claim that Republicans were making inroads with younger millennials. John Cluverius and Joshua Dyck's recent study of millennial party ID suggests that younger millennials are slightly more Republican than older members of the cohort.[8] And of course, you would expect variation within generations, because generations, particularly as defined by Pew, are social constructs. What links a baby boomer born in

1945 to the last one born at 11:59 p.m. on December 31, 1964? The former is now seventy-five years old and almost certainly retired, lived through the Vietnam War as a young person, and cast their first vote for Goldwater or Johnson. The latter couldn't vote in a presidential election until Reagan-Mondale and is likely just now reaching the pinnacle of their professional career. What even is a generation, anyway? Do the doctors and nurses, when holding the first baby of a new generation, announce, "This baby here we will call Generation Z. It will host potlucks instead of dinner parties and prefer TikTok to Twitter."

But the claim that younger millennials were getting a bit more conservative than their older counterparts is being smothered by President Trump and the Republicans. Just as the Iraq War and the Great Recession permanently drove a large segment of older millennials away from Republicans and into the waiting arms of Democrats, so too has the nonstop trauma of the Trump Era created yet another generation of forever Democrats, young people so repulsed by the unseemly antics, misogynist ravings, and racist policies of today's Republican Party that many of them are unlikely to ever consider voting for Team Red at all.

It is not yet clear that the economic and social mayhem of the COVID-19 crisis will be as bad for the Trump administration as the Iraq War or the Great Recession was for George W. Bush, but the cumulative sense of constant crisis and incompetence may be leading to the same outcome in terms of party preferences. The best evidence we have that the temporary dip in Democratic fortunes prior to the 2016 presidential election has been reversed is the results of the 2018 midterms. Of the eighteen-to-twenty-nine-year-old cohort that voted by 35 points for Democrats in House races, more than half (twenty-two-to-twenty-nine-year-olds) are the younger millennials alleged to have made a turn to the GOP in 2016. What we were seeing, most likely, was a temporary spike in support for third parties and younger millennials identifying as independents driven by the extraordinary negativity of the 2016 election, the failure of Hillary Clinton to win these voters over and perhaps some lasting resentment that Bernie Sanders did not capture the Democratic nomination. It is also worth noting that Pew's post-election reconstruction of the electorate found Trump losing the eighteen-to-twenty-nine vote much more decisively (58–28 to be exact) than the network-sponsored exit polls.

When looking at party identification, it is important to do a few things. One, while these identities are sticky, they are not nearly as permanent or ingrained as something like gender, racial, or ethnic identity. People do change their expressed party ID. Most of the fluctuation in these numbers, however, comes from nominal Independents floating in and out of the Democratic and Republican pools depending on circumstances and events. That's also why you will generally see two different numbers. Gallup frequently reports numbers that look like this:

	REPUBLICANS	INDEPENDENTS	DEMOCRATS
2019 Sept 3–15	29	38	31
2019 Aug 15–30	26	42	30
2019 Aug 1–14	27	40	29
2019 Jul 15–31	26	41	30
2019 Jul 1–12	29	38	27

In politics, as of today, do you consider yourself a Republican, a Democrat, or an independent?

Note that the proportion of people who considered themselves to be independent is higher in each case than those who considered themselves Republicans or Democrats. In fact, according to Gallup, it's really been a minute since either party had an edge on independents—2012, to be exact, when Democrats edged out independents days before the presidential election that pitted incumbent Democrat Barack Obama against Republican Mitt Romney. At one point in 2014, 47 percent of Americans said they were independent. Except, they aren't truly independents. That's why both Pew and Gallup produce a separate set of numbers which combines self-identified Democrats and Republicans and "leaners." Nearly everyone who says they are a political independent gravitates more toward one party over the other and generally votes for that party's candidates in national elections, even while expressing antipathy toward the party itself or perhaps casting a grudging vote. It is worth noting that the independents number has made a long, slow march downward at the approach of each presidential election since 2004, as party IDs become more salient and activated with the increased attention paid to the upcoming election. In any case, the data that includes leaners is much more indicative of the state of play than the one that is reported without it. Despite the large number of Americans who self-identify as politically independent, Democratic and Republican candidates continue to dominate presidential politics. Third-party candidates have not drawn more than 5.7 percent of the vote in any of the presidential elections since 2000. So that 35 percent or so of the voting public that self-identifies as independent nevertheless turns up on election day and votes for the Democratic or the Republican nominee.

The other way to look at the plight of the GOP with younger voters has nothing to do with how they self-identify, but instead how they vote on election day. And in that regard, the Republican Party is in even more trouble with millennials and Gen Zers than they are in terms of party ID. The chart below shows the eighteen-to-twenty-nine pool votes for the House since 2000. The third column reflects the election's overall results in the popular vote. The "swing" is how much more Democratic eighteen-to-twenty-nine-year-olds have voted than the overall result.

	DEMOCRAT	REPUBLICAN	RESULTS	SWING
2000	51	49	D + 0	+2
2002	51	49	R + 6	+8
2004	56	44	D + 0	+12
2006	61	39	D +8	+14
2008	65	35	D+10	+20
2010	58	42	R + 8	+24
2012	60	38	D + 1	+21
2014	55	45	R +6	+16
2016	56	42	R +1	+15
2018	67	32	D +8	+27

Since then, eighteen-to-twenty-nine-year-olds have voted anywhere from 12 points more Democratic (2004) to 27 points more Democratic (2018) than the overall electorate. It happened in good years for Democrats (2008) and bad years for Democrats (2014). And when turnout among eighteen-to-twenty-nine-year-olds has been highest, Democrats have performed well. When it falls off the map, as it did in 2010, Democrats get crushed despite overperforming with younger voters by spectacular margins. And because this has been going on for so long, the Democrats' advantage has filtered up into the next age tier. Thirty-to-forty-four-year-olds voted for Democrats by 19 points in 2018 and for Hillary Clinton by 10 points in 2016, both better than the 7-point advantage they held with that age cohort in the close 2012 election and a complete reversal of George W. Bush's 7-point win with thirty-to-forty-nine-year-olds in 2004. Time keeps marching on. Some of the thirty-to-forty-four-year-olds from 2016 will be washing up in the forty-five-to-sixty-four sample in 2020. And a whole new cohort of eighteen-to-twenty-two-year-olds who were ineligible to vote in 2016 will participate in the 2020 elections. All indications so far are that they will decisively vote against President Trump, assuming he limps along in office to the conclusion of his first term. At that point the span of the oldest voter from the original left-leaning eighteen-to-twenty-nine-year-old cohort in 2002 to the youngest left-leaning voter in 2020 will be nearly thirty years long. And for the first time there will be more of this group as a share of the electorate than the combined total of boomers and members of the Silent Generation. If you throw in the very modestly left-leaning Generation X (born between 1965 and 1980), you have a model in which right-leaning voters are quite decisively outnumbered by the left-leaning ones.

This has created a situation in which very few observers, and even fewer polls, give Donald Trump any shot whatsoever of winning more raw votes in the 2020 election. The Republicans' presidential hopes lie almost exclusively in hoping he can pull off another victory in the Electoral College by capturing one or more of Wisconsin, Pennsylvania, and

Michigan, and keeping the rest of the map the same. Current polling at the time of this writing suggests that there is certainly a significant chance the GOP will succeed in holding on to the presidency in this dubiously democratic fashion. But the damage to the long-term fortunes of Republicans of having Donald Trump be the party figurehead for another four years will far outweigh whatever fleeting policy benefits the party can consolidate before even the tipping-point Electoral College states drift into the Democratic column.

Many Republicans seem to be counting on the Electoral College to misfire repeatedly, or they are counting on the Senate, where Republicans might be able to cling to power for the foreseeable future. This would be a mistake. While Democrats aren't winning the youth vote everywhere, the GOP should be terrified of the electoral implications of the state-by-state exit polls in 2016 and 2018. Young Texans, for instance, voted Clinton 55–36 in 2016, and for Senate candidate Beto O'Rourke over Republican Ted Cruz by a staggering 42 points in 2018 (71–29). The slow drip of poll numbers showing Democratic candidates running competitively with President Trump in Texas in 2020 are an omen of things to come there. Without the more than thirty electoral votes (more after the 2020 census) Texas has reliably provided to the GOP coalition for two generations, the Republican path to the presidency becomes nearly impassable. Flipping Texas in 2016 *alone* would have provided Hillary Clinton with a two-electoral-vote victory. With Trump, Wisconsin, Michigan, and Pennsylvania are likely to lose Congressional seats and therefore electoral votes after 2020. Texas will take on an even more pivotal role in presidential politics.

It's not just Texas. Across the rapidly growing Sun Belt, Democrats are slaughtering Republicans with younger voters. Of the twenty-six states for which we have 2016 exit polling data, Democrats won the eighteen-to-twenty-nine vote in 22 of them, including sun-soaked battlegrounds like North Carolina (57–35), Florida (54–36), Georgia (63–33), and Arizona (53–35). Of the eighteen states with exit polling for a Senate race in the 2018 midterms, Republicans lost the youngest demographic in all of them. Throw in the 2017 Alabama Senate race in which Democrat Doug Jones won youngsters by 22 points, and it's nineteen states. Throw in the Georgia governor's race, and Democrats went 20 for 20 with this group. And in the Kyrsten Sinema (D) and Martha McSally (R) race in Arizona, we only have data for eighteen-to-forty-four-year-olds, but Democrats won those too. Granted, 2018 was a wave election year for Democrats, but the margins should give GOP elites real pause. Democrat Phil Bredeson, for instance, beat Republican Marcia Blackburn with this set by 39 points (69–30). In Montana, Democrat Jon Tester won the youngest voters by 38 points. In Georgia, Democratic gubernatorial candidate Stacey Abrams crushed Brian Kemp by 29. In Florida, Democrat Bill Nelson, a truly underwhelming incumbent candidate, carried the youth vote 66–32. These are states Republicans simply cannot afford to kick away if they intend to cling to power in the Senate or miracle their way to another Electoral College victory without the popular vote. Trends in the youth vote should be especially worrisome in presumed Republican landslide states like Tennessee, Montana, and Missouri, where Democratic Senator Claire McCaskill won eighteen-to-twenty-nine-year-olds even while being thrown out of office. Democrats also narrowly won the youngest voters in the Mississippi Senate race.

In fact, digging through this data, there isn't really any state that isn't already a landslide Republican stronghold where you can say that the demographics are moving in the right direction for the GOP. The current 53–47 Republican Senate advantage is built on the party's structural advantage with smaller, rural states, combined with enduring strength in populous, thriving Sun Belt states like Georgia, North Carolina, Florida, Texas, and Arizona. Those five states, as of this writing, have 9 Republican senators and 1 Democratic senator. Even in Rust Belt states where Trump outperformed recent Republican presidential nominees, there is precious little good news. Young voters went for Trump 48–42 in Iowa, which is something. He nearly won them in Wisconsin, losing by just 3 points. He also came close in Minnesota with the same 3-point deficit in a state that was won by Clinton in unexpectedly dramatic fashion. But coming close isn't winning. And that competitiveness vanished in 2018, when Democratic gubernatorial candidate Tony Evers beat incumbent Scott Walker with young voters 60–37, with the same story playing out in Minnesota's two Senate races. Same deal in Pennsylvania, where incumbent Bob Casey crushed it with the kids, 61–37. The only state where swapping out over sixty-fives with younger voters would benefit the Republican Party is Maine, where, according to the exit polls, the oldest Mainers provided Clinton's statewide margin of victory in 2016. We'll certainly have more data on that after the 2020 presidential election, with both Republican incumbent Susan Collins and Trump on the ballot. My hunch is that the Maine data in the 2016 exits was a little fluky, and even then, it's not like Trump *won* the youngest voters. He just didn't get walloped by them.

Apart from exit polls, the only other state-level data we have for the Republican future comes from the Scholastic mock presidential election. Laugh all you want, but there is data here from a jaw-dropping 153,000 K–12 students in the United States. In 2016, Hillary Clinton beat Donald Trump in this poll by 17 points, 52–35, with an unusually high number of students opting to write in real (Gary Johnson) or joke (Bacon) third-party candidates. The Democratic advantage with this group is likely even greater than 17 points, as 2016 was an outlier in terms of the number of votes cast for third-party candidates, despite all of the preelection media hectoring about the dangers of doing so.[9] Even so, Clinton won thirty-four states, plus DC, to just sixteen for Trump.

SCHOLASTIC YOUTH VOTE MAP, 2016 ELECTION

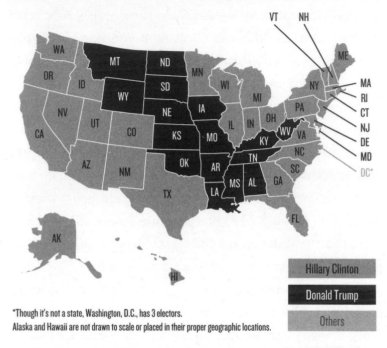

*Though it's not a state, Washington, D.C., has 3 electors.
Alaska and Hawaii are not drawn to scale or placed in their proper geographic locations.

Clinton won this particular youth vote basically every-where except the Gulf Coast and parts of the interior.

The battleground state data was especially grim. Clinton won by 9 in North Carolina and Florida.[10] She came out on top by 19 points in New Hampshire. Only in Iowa (where Trump won by a point), Ohio (where Clinton won by that same point), and maybe Wisconsin (where Clinton was only up by 6) do we see any information from critical states that should give GOP elites a sense of optimism about the future. But Iowa is already lost to the GOP, and Wisconsin's numbers don't seem bad enough to project it as being anything less than an important swing state for the next generation, albeit perhaps a Republican leaning one. Clinton also won Texas, North Carolina and South Carolina, Georgia, and Arizona, all places projected to experience the most population growth over the next decade.

To give Republicans some hope that this situation will not eventually turn out very bad for them would require us to see significant movement toward Republicans in some number of states that are currently counted in the Democratic column. You might think to look in some of the whitest states (like Maine) to see whether any of them are still Democratic and whether they might be trending away toward the GOP. There's not much help coming here either. The fifteen states with the highest percentage of non-Hispanic whites are already represented by twenty-two Republican senators, six Democrats, and two independents who caucus with the liberal side. The major outliers right now are New Hampshire, Vermont, and Minnesota, all heavily white states that nevertheless supply six Democrats to the US Senate. While we have no data on how young Vermonters voted in the past two elections, the overall data does not support the idea that the state will trend right simply because of its racial makeup. The Republican share of the Vermont vote in presidential election years has dropped from 40.7 percent in 2000 to just 29.8 percent in 2016. Minnesota gave Democrats a scare in 2016, and eighteen-to-twenty-nine-year-olds only went for Clinton 45–42. But Democrats won both of their 2018 Senate

races in the state going away, with incumbent Amy Klobuchar winning by 24 points and Tina Smith, appointed to Al
Franken's seat earlier that year, by 11. Young Minnesotans
went for Smith by 27 points. Even factoring in the Democratic wave dynamics, these are not numbers which support
the idea of Minnesota suddenly becoming lean-Republican.
In fact, Minnesota has never been the blowout Democratic
state that we might imagine it to be as part of its status as a
Blue Wall stronghold. The state went for Gore by just 2.4 percent in 2000. Only in 2008 did Democrats really blow it out
there, with Obama winning by 11.

That leaves New Hampshire. A longstanding swing state,
Granite Staters nevertheless lean Democratic. New Hampshire went narrowly for Bush in 2000 before voting narrowly
against him in 2004. Like Minnesota, Obama exploded the
doors off the hinges in 2008. In 2012, Obama won the state
by 5.6, and then Clinton eked out a win of less than half a
point in 2016. In theory, this means the state could be shifting
against Democrats. And we have no follow-up data to work
with from 2018. But it's worth noting that even in the 2016
squeaker, Clinton won eighteen-to-twenty-nine-year-old
New Hampshirans by 8 points.

What if, instead of whiteness, we looked at another factor that has more and more come to divide the population
between Democrats and Republicans: higher education. The
education gap, as it has come to be known, will be discussed
more fully in chapter 4. In 2016, Clinton won voters with a

college degree by 10 points, 52–42, and lost those without one by 7 points, 51–44. This has led some analysts to speculate that Democrats are in the most trouble in states with low percentages of college graduates. Again though, the data isn't especially promising for Republicans. Of the fifteen states with the lowest percentage of college degree-holders, Republicans already hold twenty-five of the thirty Senate seats. Of those five Democrats, one is West Virginia's Joe Manchin, the most conservative Democrat in the chamber and a major party-switching risk, and another is Doug Jones, who captured one of Alabama's seats in a 2017 special election mostly because Republican primary voters insisted on nominating a credibly accused pederast named Roy Moore.

We don't have data for heavily Republican states like Louisiana, Idaho, South Dakota, or Kansas. But the implications of the data we do have are pretty clear—growing states with more diverse youth populations are trending quickly Democratic, and Republicans may be minimizing if not reversing their losses in shrinking, heavily white states like Wisconsin, Maine, Iowa, and Ohio. If true, Republicans are in much more serious long-term trouble in places like Mississippi and Alabama than they are in white strongholds like Wyoming and West Virginia. The youngest Americans, ages zero to seventeen in 2016, were 75 percent or more white in just eleven states. Across the old confederacy, whites make up less than 60 percent of the population. The situation, frankly, looks quite grim for the future of the Republican Party.

It is important to highlight how unusual this situation is in the polling era. In the recent past, it was unusual for the choice of any age demographic group to diverge this much from the overall result in a presidential election year. In the four elections from 1984 to 1996, all age demographics voted for the winner. This was close to being true in 1980 as well, when Jimmy Carter very narrowly carried eighteen-to-twenty-one-year-olds by a point. None of these were especially close elections, but the absence of a huge generational split is noticeable. Even in the extraordinarily close 2000 election, no age group differed from the 48–48 baseline by more than four points. It should go without saying that prior to this century neither Democrats nor Republicans scored dramatic victories with particular age groups—in comparison to the overall vote—in multiple national elections in a row. In other words, the generation gap is completely new, and very poorly understood.

It is also just . . . massive. The Democrats' 35-point win with eighteen-to-twenty-nine-year-olds in 2018 was the largest victory either party scored with any age cohort since 1972, when Democrat George McGovern won just 30 percent of forty-six-to-sixty-one-year-olds and 32 percent of sixty-two-to-seventy-seven-year-olds, according to data from the American National Election Studies.[11] In fact, in all of the ANES data, there are only a few points as bad as 2018 for either party with any age demographic at all, most from the blowout, landslide elections of 1964 and 1972. There are a few outliers from older elections—Democrat Harry Truman won 70 percent of eighteen-to-twenty-one-year-olds in 1948, for instance. But the data is generally pretty consistent. It is important to note that the Silent Generation has always been all over the place. In 1952, 57 percent went for Republican Dwight Eisenhower. In 1964, 70 percent went for Democrat Lyndon Johnson. As political scientists will tell you, these numbers were the product of ideological closeness between the two parties in this time period, with many Democrats in Congress more conservative than the most liberal Republicans and vice versa. But beginning in 1976, America entered a period where voting behavior between the generations became much more consistent. For instance, Americans born between 1975 and 1990 have given Democrats anywhere from 56 percent of their votes (1992) to 66 percent (2004).

Part of the misunderstanding of these consequential numbers relates to popular misperceptions about what happens to people's beliefs and partisanship as they age. More on that in chapter 3. But even people who know the dynamics of these things pretty well are missing the forest for the trees. In 2017, Deborah Schildtkraut, the chair of the political science department at Tufts, tried to knock down the conventional wisdom about the GOP's problems with young people. She noted that "the gap between different age groups that emerged in the early 2000s has stabilized. There is no clear downward trend in Republican identification among young people."[12] Two points here: one, this has been proven untrue by events subsequent to 2017 and is a cautionary tale about drawing conclusions from one data point in time. The GOP may have succeeded in wrapping a tourniquet around its open wound with young voters in the second half of the Obama administration, but Trump has ripped it right off. More importantly, even if the generation gap from early aughts was set in stone from now until the end of time, with Republicans capturing the same share of future generations as they did with young millennials, that would be *completely catastrophic* for them.

Imagine an entire voting-eligible population characterized in its entirety by the partisan leanings and ideological proclivities of the millennials and Gen Zers. In this world, the millennials are the elderly, still voting for Democrats by double digits. The Generation Zers are in early to late middle age. Remember, too, the iron law of American voting that shows the elderly turning out in higher numbers than young folks. I have no idea what Pew will end up calling the post-post-millennials, but for the sake of argument, let's call them the Coastal Flooding Generation. If that generation is even remotely as left-leaning as its predecessors, the Republican Party could literally go extinct, be replaced by an ideological rival that can better reflect what would be the center-right on the emerging ideological spectrum, or drift along losing most national elections by pretty catastrophic numbers.

But the kids won't be left forever, right? Can the younger generations' commitment to high-tax Scandinavian social democracy really survive sustained contact with property tax raises and socialized medicine? Didn't the free-love Wood-stock generation of the 1960s eventually become one of the more hardened Republican constituencies in American politics? While it rarely gets the attention of the latest horse-race polling or presidential favorability numbers, there is a copious amount of research about how people acquire their partisanship and how it does or does not change over time. And very little of it should give much hope to conservatives that today's young leftists will age into tomorrow's rock-ribbed Republican loyalists.

CHAPTER 3

THE KIDS AREN'T GETTING MORE CONSERVATIVE

AMONG THE MANY rogues, grifters, and scallywags that comprise the far-right media universe, there is one name that would genuinely shock someone who had been in a coma since the 1960s: David Horowitz. A prominent student radical and founding intellectual of the New Left, the now-eighty-year-old Horowitz once edited the far-left magazine *Ramparts*, was known as a combative firebrand, and struck up a friendship with Black Panther Huey Newton. His parents were Marxists. But when Horowitz suspected that some of his radical friends were implicated in the murder of his friend Betty Van Patter, he began to drift away from the movement, first to a more centrist liberalism and then finally to Ronald Reagan's GOP in the 1980s. Horowitz brought his execute-all-prisoners style to the right, founding the "David

Horowitz Freedom Center," perhaps best known for vituper-
ative anti-Islamic and anti-immigrant rhetoric that presaged
the rise of outlets like *Breitbart* and the *Daily Caller*. Horowitz, a man who is virtually unknown to normal people but
nevertheless quite influential on the right, built an exceed-
ingly seedy empire by preying on the fears of older white
Americans, exploiting the Islamophobic panic that gripped
the United States after 9/11 and then, naturally, aligning
himself with the MAGA movement.

To most people, this remarkable transformation—from
rigid leftist ideologue to bomb-throwing right-winger—might
seem extreme but not atypical. That's why people are always
tossing that "if you're not a liberal when you're twenty-five"
aphorism around like it means something. Young people can
be dreamers with no responsibilities, but once you're deep
into a mortgage and car payments staring down the muzzle
of college tuition for your kids and saving for retirement, you
start to want those tax cuts. The widespread belief that young
Alexandria Ocasio-Cortezes turn into cranky Archie Bunkers
as they get older is primarily caused by something called the
"availability heuristic," that is, the tendency of human beings
to rely on familiar examples when making judgements.

One such example would be my own dad, who went from
writing a book called *Revisionist Marxism* in 1973 to voting
twice for George W. Bush.[1] His political transformation (it is
important to note that despite our political differences, he is
an incredible father and person and I sincerely hope that he

has made it this far in the book) is probably the first thing that comes to mind for everyone in our extended family when we consider the subject of shifting partisan loyalties.

Daniel Oppenheimer, who chronicled Horowitz's transformation as part of his book *Exit Right*, believes that the movement from left-to right tells us something important about the twentieth century and about ourselves. "The stories are worth telling," he says, "because it's during the period of political transition, when the bones of one's belief system are broken and poking out through the skin, that the contingency and complexity of belief become most visible."[2] He urges us "to recognize that political belief, if we're to act on it, should be hard-earned." The book is premised on the idea that things change, "people change," as he puts it, and "pieces of people change."[3] That's true, for sure, but Oppenheimer's book is impoverished by the lack of any social scientific evidence. He doesn't cite a single political scientist to help understand the life journeys of the six men he chronicles. The words "party ID" do not appear at all. And that failure, to systematize our understanding of personal political change, is something Oppenheimer shares with the general culture, which assumes a kind of political fluidity in most people which simply does not exist.

The study of voter behavior is one of the oldest and most dense endeavors in the field of political science. Why do people make the choices they do at the ballot box? What causes the sometimes dramatic, sometimes nearly imperceptible changes in party preference between elections? What can parties do to appeal to voters, to turn out people who rarely or never vote, and to appeal to those who lack firm ideological or partisan preferences? These questions apply both to the forces of any given election, but also and more importantly for our purposes, to the long-term dynamics of party loyalty and ideology. In a vacuum, I think most people would assume that voters are purely rational actors, who approach each election from a cost-benefit and values standpoint, diligently researching and processing the candidates' platforms and making an informed judgment independent of nearly all other variables. Your preferences are, in the political science lingo, rank-ordered. Maybe your most important concerns are health care, inequality, racial injustice, terrorism, and the deficit, in that order. If that seems like an odd mix, stay tuned. The point is that these are your most important issues, in that exact order, and that you'll make your choices by how well the candidates fit your preference assortment.

These assumptions are actually quite deeply ingrained in our political culture. Exit pollsters frequently ask people to rank which issues were most important to them, and pundits and analysts use those results to determine which party had the best election strategy. On election night in 2004, for example, voters leaving the polls told exit pollsters that "moral values" was the most important issue to them, and a thousand wretched hot takes bloomed about how Democrats needed to win over "family values" voters if they were going to avoid being condemned to permanent minority status.[4] Before it became clear that George W. Bush's radioactivity was going to doom the GOP in the next two elections, this debate and its consequences consumed an unbelievable share of Democratic energy.

And sometimes, no one agrees about which issue was most important to voters. In the aftermath of the 2018 midterms, Democrats claimed that Republican efforts to sabotage the Affordable Care Act cost them their House majority, while Republicans argued that Democratic opposition to the nomination of Brett Kavanaugh to the Supreme Court led to the GOP expanding its margins in the upper chamber. On the one hand, you have millions of people looking at candidates and voting blue to preserve their preexisting conditions protections. On the other, millions are enraged about Brett Kavanaugh's terrible treatment at the hands of Senate Democrats and decide to pull the lever for Team Red after all.

It will probably not surprise you by now to learn that political scientists take a pretty dim view of both of these narratives. Most normal people do not begin each election cycle like LeBron James splashing the market, as pure free agents, equally available to any political party capable of soliciting their votes and convincing them that their issue-positions are the best ones. There may be a relatively small pool of voters who behave something like this, but ironically, they are probably the ones who pay the least attention to politics and make up their minds at something close to the very last second in exact ways that would probably drive anyone reading this book completely insane.

If I were to do the math on my own family, Dad is the outlier. Mom is from a large family of liberal Kentucky Catholics, some of whom have gotten *more* progressive as they aged. My late Uncle Ben, who I remember from childhood as insouciant and politically incorrect, became an ardent conservationist who donated money to the Southern Poverty Law Center and had multiple pictures of Barack Obama on the walls of the small home he shared in Somerset, Kentucky, with my aunt Libby. On my dad's side, Uncle Gerald and all of his kids grew up liberal and remain stridently so, whereas Uncle Steve has always been conservative.

So our family is fairly typical of how partisans age, and this is true of both self-identified Democrats and self-identified Independents. Take my brother Jason, for instance. An accomplished oncologist, he has always been repulsed by some of the more craven aspects of party politics and is attracted in principle to the idea of bipartisanship. He mulled over voting for Republican Scott Brown in the 2012 Massachusetts Senate race, although he did eventually pull the lever for Elizabeth Warren. Then in 2016 he supported Bernie Sanders in the Democratic primary. As he got older, rather than growing more conservative as he acquired property, started a family and moved up the income ladder, he got more progressive in many ways, worrying in particular about what would be left of the planet his four children would inherit. His voting pattern is pretty typical for what political scientists call "lean-ers"—people who do not express loyalty to either party but who are clearly more aligned with one of them and vote as such most of the time.

To sum up: In my family, out of my one sibling, two parents, nine aunts and uncles, and seventeen cousins, there appears to be only one or two people who vote for a different party than they did when they were young adults. And it turns out that we are pretty typical. We have a lot of data, and very little of it is friendly to the idea that the Republican Party will shortly be rescued from oblivion by millennials who decide that they love tax cuts, deregulation, and virulent bigotry after all.

This is not at all what the architects of the American constitution intended, but it turns out that most people are, wittingly or unwittingly, intense partisan loyalists, whose voting preferences are largely predetermined long before the candidates drop millions of dollars on last-minute ad blitzes. The political scientist Rachel Bitecofer famously calls the idea of persuadable swing voters "The Chuck Todd Theory of Politics" and argues instead that elections are won and lost by how many of your own partisans are sufficiently motivated by "negative partisanship" (fear and loathing of the other party) show up on election day.[5] Those partisan loyalties, much more so than even the recent past, can predict with great precision which party's candidate you will vote for in federal races (less so for offices like governor and attorney general, but certainly more so than a generation ago). And so for the past long generation, electoral outcomes have depended mostly on a few factors that are completely independent of a candidate's ability to persuade fair-thinking people of the merits of their arguments.

First, those outcomes have depended on the degree to which each party's more marginal loyalists care enough about the election itself to turn out. The election of Donald Trump, for instance, seems to have depended on slightly depressed turnout among critical Democratic constituencies in a small handful of states along with unusually high defections to third parties, especially among young people. Second, in particularly close races, the choices of pure independent voters, the ones who genuinely do not lean toward one party or another, were decisive. Neither factor in isolation can explain outcomes. In 2012, for example, Republican nominee Mitt Romney actually won self-identified Independents yet lost the election narrowly to incumbent President Barack Obama, whose unique personal appeal drove massive turnout from the party's base and allowed him to hold on to a broad but narrow victory. On the other hand, when independents line up with one candidate and that candidate also turns out his or her core supporters in significant numbers, you get the kind of blowout that has become increasingly rare in American presidential politics.

This is what happened in 2008, when Obama crushed Republican John McCain with Independents and also mobilized incredible youth and minority turnout to win the election handily. His overall popular vote share was the highest seen in elections since 1988. In the polarized environment that had characterized national American politics since 1988, Obama's blowout was rare. And with each party boasting a similar-sized partisan core, the assumption has long been that this era of close elections will continue indefinitely.

But that's not what's on the horizon. And pervasive misperceptions about what drives voter behavior are at the heart of why the coming political transformation in America is not more widely understood. In fact, we are already quite far into that transformation. Party loyalists are, if anything, even more committed to voting for candidates from their tribe than ever before. Elections, if nothing else, have been incredibly close. So what is changing? In short: young voters are becoming Democratic party loyalists in unprecedented numbers. Nothing in the field of political science really should give any hope to Republicans that their loyalties will shift right in the long duree.

Political science is less of a science than its most intense practitioners would like to think. But when it comes to how people vote and which parties they are loyal to, the field has produced real insights. Social scientists have been collecting data throughout the post-WWII period, and while there isn't total agreement about every little detail, I can safely convey with confidence the following findings to you: One, people don't get more conservative as they age. If anything, the older people get the more likely they are to double down on partisan loyalties and dismiss information that doesn't fit with their partisanship. Two, committed partisans don't generally switch teams. Adults who change partisanship have typically gone through one of a small number of disjunctive life events, like a divorce or a move far away from home that embeds them in a very different kind of community.[6] Politically speaking, millennials and Gen Zers are unlikely to have the kinds of rare life experiences that might cause them to drift to the right in significant enough numbers to change what's happening. And if we were looking dispassionately at the data rather than fixating on a small number of high-profile cases of political conversion from left to right, we would already know this. And Republicans would be even more terrified than they already are.

In fact, most people's partisan preferences harden in early adulthood, and children tend to inherit their parents' partisan preferences—as long as both parents share it. The process of acquiring specific views about politics is known in academic circles as *political socialization*. And the process obviously involves more than parents' views—friends, geographic location, teachers, neighborhoods, and even one-off events like 9/11 or Watergate can help shape the political leanings of young people. When social scientists talk about these things, it's important to remember that we're looking at probabilities rather than certainties. There is no law of political gravity that says if both your parents were Republicans you will be too. It's just *more likely*.

When I was an elementary school student in south Jersey in the mid-1980s, I marched into class every day with an almost burning hatred of President Ronald Reagan. Our Little League T-ball squads were organized into two teams—Republicans and Democrats (a practice that seems like it would be an invitation to town-wide mayhem today). What did I know about politics? Precious little. I was a seven-year-old kid with a Scooby-Doo obsession and backpack full of textbooks carefully decorated with the Beatles logo, and I spent most of my spare time reading science fiction and watching baseball. What fleeting morsels of information I did know about politics came from my parents, and my parents were, at the time, a pair of Democrats whose partisanship was so open that they used to put signs out on our lawn for municipal and state elections. Our most frequent out-of-town visitors were my dad's advisor from the University Bridgeport, a doctrinaire communist named David DeGrood, who left behind a ten-volume history of the twentieth century when he died, and his wife Elaine. For most seven-year-olds, there isn't anyone in the world to trust more than your parents, and so I was a Democrat in the same way that I loved the New York Mets and St. Louis Cardinals, because that's what my brother was into. But the label stuck. I was a Democrat when I was a kid and a Democrat when I was a teenager and a Democrat when I voted in my first election, the 1994 midterms, and a Democrat when I graduated from college in 2000 and a Democrat when I got married in 2013 and a Democrat after my son was born in 2018. And here you are,

reading a book written by a lifelong forty-two-year-old Democrat who will take that partisanship to the grave.

I'm not special at all. The existing research is pretty clear:
if your parents share the same partisanship, you are likely to
hold those views throughout your entire life. This is known as
"intergenerational agreement."[7] A group of Stanford researchers found in 2018 that children of same-partisanship families
since 1965 have had nearly a 75 percent chance of expressing
that same partisanship. This shouldn't be surprising. Especially
for young children, your parents constitute a huge percentage
of your overall universe. We unconsciously adopt all kinds of
habits and ideas from our parents, and politics is no different. The statistical effect is increased the more that parents
speak about politics in front of their kids. That makes intrinsic
sense—after all, children have very few opportunities to think
about or learn about politics. The more they hear their parents
revealing their political attitudes and beliefs in conversation,
the more likely they are to pick up on those cues and adopt that
thinking as their own. Fascinatingly, studies also show that
kids can adopt the wrong partisanship, by mistakenly attribut-
ing a partisanship to their parents they do not actually possess.

Looking at longitudinal data, they also found that people
are significantly more likely to be married to partners who
share their political outlook than they were fifty years ago.
In 1965, that number was about 74.2 percent. Today it is 81.5
percent. In other words, more than four out of five couples are
comprised of two people who share the same partisanship.
Either the supply of different-party partners is quite limited

in specific areas (not a surprise given the accelerated dynamics of partisan sorting), or people are deliberately excluding potential partners from the other party from their dating pool. Researchers tend to agree that this remarkable result is driven today more by intentional choice than by anything else.[8] Let me put it this way—I saw more than a few profiles in my OkCupid dating days in the mid-2000s in which the person said some variation of "Republicans need not apply."[9]

So there's another thing that makes my dad's story an outlier—his wife, my mom, has remained quite liberal into her seventies, and has done volunteer work for Democratic candidates in the past several national election cycles. Social scientists have looked at the role of spouses on political attitudes. After all, aside from your parents, a spouse is the longest-standing and most intimate relationship a person might ever have. And while the amount of time spent with parents declines precipitously once people leave home, most will spend dozens of hours a week or more with their spouse until the day one of them dies. Under those circumstances, it is almost impossible not to imagine there being some kind of congruence between political attitudes, if only to keep the peace. My parents adore each other, but my mom does sometimes say to him something like, "I love you, Ralph, but I did prefer it when you were a communist."

Here, scholars are somewhat split. On one hand, some researchers clearly believe that spouses who might initially have different political attitudes influence each other politically over time. As political scientist Amanda Williams wrote in a 2004 study, "marriage, and the opportunities that marriage allows for political discussion among partners, do impact partners' political views and partisanship."[10] Another study found that while about 72 percent of recently married couples agree about politics, more than 82 percent of those who have been married for two decades or longer share partisanship.[11] Jeffrey Lyons, looking at the Youth-Parent Socialization Study conducted in multiple waves between 1965 and 1997, found that "by age 35, the spouse is more influential than either parent was at age 18."[12] Of course, that could be caused by the marriages of disagreers falling apart as much as it is by persuasion. But there is clearly something going on here.

The most important way that midlife and late-life partisanship can shift is by being embedded in a different partisan environment. Lyons, for instance, found a statistically significant change in partisanship can be obtained by moving from more Republican to less Republican areas (and vice versa, of course).[13] If you're a Bernie-voting progressive medical student from San Francisco, and you decide to take a job in a rural area and stay there for a long time, there is a pretty good chance the social and political attitudes of your neighbors will start to rub off on you. You might make friends who rope you into hunting and change your mind about the second amendment. Or perhaps you meet, for the first time in your life, large numbers of people who are quite religious, and you become close to several of them. While you might not be born again yourself, you might also find your hostility to religious values dampen and, consciously or unconsciously, you might begin to think the arguments against things like abortion and premarital sex have some merit.

We don't have good migration data yet on post-millennials, but millennials who do move are generally leaving one metro area for another, or they are moving from cities to the suburbs of those cities.[14] Young people generally are still flocking to major metropolitan areas, particularly in the Sun Belt, as they look for career opportunities. A generation ago, the suburbs in most parts of America were reliable Republican vote-producers. But the big story of the past ten years is the rapid bluing of suburbs all around the country. While Clinton and Trump roughly split suburban voters in 2016 (getting about 37 million votes apiece), Clinton clobbered him in the inner suburbs close to metropolitan cores, the places where millennials are buying houses after getting priced out of urban housing markets.

The transformation of the suburbs is further along in some places than in others. Suburban Orange County, California, for instance, voted Democratic in 2016 for the first time since FDR's election, and in 2018 sent zero Republicans to Congress. In places like Philadelphia, Chicago, Boston, and New York, suburban Republicans have been nearly wiped out of Congress altogether. The GOP maintains some strength in farther-flung suburbs of cities like Indianapolis and Nashville, for instance. But in the growing cities of the Sun Belt, like Raleigh-Durham, North Carolina, Houston, Texas, and

Phoenix, Arizona, Democrats are making rapid gains that threaten long-standing Republican control of those states. In any case, we needn't make any precise predictions about how particular Congressional races are going to unfold to conclude that that a vanishingly small share of millennials will be moving to either Republican-dominated outer-ring suburbs, or even less likely, to rural areas from a metro region. It's also worth noting that the strength of the effect on partisanship only gets significant when voters move to an area heavily dominated by the other party—in that sense, even outer-ring suburbs, in which Trump beat Clinton by roughly 56 percent to 44 percent,[15] probably don't qualify as places that would exert an inexorable pull away from liberalism. While you probably know someone in your social circle who decamped to the middle of nowhere from a city, they are outliers. It simply won't be a significant enough trend over the next generation to make a dent in millennial and Gen Z partisanship, and it certainly won't offset the steady flow of people out of rural areas and into more robust, job-rich metro regions. So that's one avenue of partisan change basically closed off. And if 81 percent of Democrats are marrying other Democrats, there's not going to be a large-scale, marriage-driven transformation of the millennial or Generation Z electorate either.

Taking all of this research into consideration, there is perhaps even less for Republican elites to feel optimistic about than I might have thought before I dove into this particular subject. If your partisan identification is inherited as a young person from your parents, and if the only things that can shake that early socialization loose are marrying someone with very different views or moving somewhere you are badly outnumbered by opposite partisans, it is hard to see how Republicans can make a long-term comeback with millennials, post-millennials, *or* the generation to follow.

The most significant counterargument you could offer to the grip that partisanship is likely to have on millennials and Gen Zers as they age is that has been one generation that appeared to grow more conservative as time marched on. The so-called Silent Generation—those born between 1928 and 1945—has seen almost a perfect inversion of its partisanship since 1992. In that year, when Democrat Bill Clinton won his election over George H. W. Bush easily, members of the Silent Generation preferred Democrats to Republicans by a 54–38 margin. By 2018, those numbers had been reversed, with 52 percent identifying as Republican and 43 percent as Democratic.[16] This is, admittedly, an enormous and consequential shift that explains much of how Republicans have been able to eke out victories at the presidential level in 2000, 2004, and 2016. What happened? Did hard-living leftists die off earlier than their more staid counterparts? For this generation in particular, the 1960s loom particularly large. Some of the most famous converts from postwar liberalism to Reagan conservatism hail from the Silent Generation.

However, I don't think converts are emblematic of this shift. I think the person who typifies the transformation of the Silent Generation is someone whose values remained steady as the partisanship associated with them shifted from Clinton to Bush: take the late Zell Miller. In the '90s, Miller was a freshly elected governor of Georgia, part of the influential group of New Democrats seeking to wrest control of the Democratic Party from adherents of postwar liberalism. The term *New Democrats* grew out of the efforts of the Democratic Leadership Council (DLC), formed in 1985, in the aftermath of back-to-back national drubbings at the hands of Ronald Reagan and the Republicans. While Democrats managed to hold the House of Representatives even during the height of Reagan's power, many party elites could see the South in particular slipping away as white southerners began identifying with the Republican Party.[17] The DLC wasn't part of Congress, but resembled organizations like the House Freedom Caucus and the Progressive Caucus in the way it brought like-minded leaders together to change the direction of the party.

It is not a coincidence that many leading New Democrats were white southerners like Clinton, Miller, Tennessee Senator Al Gore, and Virginia Governor Chuck Robb: their geographic commonality was part of the appeal, and part of the project of preserving Democratic power in the Deep South, which was finally beginning to slip away after surviving, particularly in state politics, for two decades after white southerners began voting Republican in presidential elections in the 1960s. Several prominent members of the DLC, including Gore, Senator Joe Biden of Delaware, and Representative Dick Gephardt of

Missouri, sought the party's nomination in 1988, only to see it won by another New Deal liberal Massachusetts Governor Michael Dukakis. When Dukakis lost badly to George H. W. Bush, it gave new momentum to the DLC and its leaders, who were calling themselves New Democrats. The DLC had, until that point, failed to offer a robust set of policy alternatives to those who had led Democrats to defeat in three consecutive presidential elections, the first time either party had dropped more than two in a row since the 1940s. DLC leaders decided that they needed to spearhead an "ideas movement."[18]

Those ideas—including a focus on balanced budgets, fighting crime, economic growth—allowed the party to capture the presidency in 1992 behind the young governor of Arkansas, Bill Clinton. The DLC's new prominence in party politics was why Miller was granted a prominent spot at the convention that year. "That this kind of voice could travel here from a forgotten corner of Appalachia," he told the audience at the 1992 Democratic National Convention in New York City, "is a testament to the grace of God, and the greatness of the Democratic Party." He extolled, of course, the virtues of Bill Clinton and Al Gore, but also genuflected to the history of the party: "My family would still be isolated and destitute if we had not had FDR's Democratic brand of government."[19]

Miller was considered by party leadership to be a star, a future senator or perhaps even a presidential or vice presidential candidate. And indeed, he ran for, and captured, one of Georgia's Senate seats in 2000 after being appointed to the seat of the late Paul Coverdell in 1999 by Democratic Governor Roy Barnes. He won a resounding 20-point victory over his Republican opponent, Mack Mattingly. He was also the last Democrat to win a Senate race in Georgia up to the time of this writing. Beginning in the early 2000s, the state fell deeply into the grip of the conservative right, completing a journey that, like in many places across the Deep South, began with providing Republicans electoral votes in presidential elections that presaged a total takeover of state politics many years later.

After his election to the Senate, Miller's relationship with his fellow Democrats quickly deteriorated. In 2003, he published a memoir called *A National Party No More: The Conscience of a Conservative Democrat*. And then, in a move that infuriated Democrats across the country, he endorsed incumbent President George W. Bush and spoke at the Republican National Convention in 2004. "I can remember when Democrats believed it was the duty of America to fight for freedom over tyranny," a seething Miller told the crowd. "Today's Democratic leaders see America as an occupier, not a liberator." He lit into Democratic nominee John Kerry at length, arguing that "no pair has been more wrong, more loudly, more often than the two Senators from Massachusetts, Ted Kennedy and John Kerry."[20] Miller's presence at the convention was a spectacle that gave Americans the impression that Bush had bipartisan support and helped give conservative Democrats permission to cross the aisle and vote to reelect Bush. Bush won 11 percent of Democratic voters, while Kerry won just 6 percent of Republicans. That was the difference in a very close election that Bush won by just 2.4 points, 50.7 percent to 48.3 percent. Had Kerry earned 118,000 more votes in Ohio, he would have been the second consecutive president to take office after losing the popular vote.

Miller was a difficult figure to pin down. He didn't run again for the Senate in 2004, and late in life, he endorsed Democrat Michelle Dunn in her Senate race against Republican David Perdue. But his slow drift from lifelong Democrat to virtual party-switcher tracks closely with trends in his generation. Born in 1932 and raised in the shadow of New Deal liberalism, Miller was an early opponent, like many southern Democrats, of civil rights legislation.[21] And while he later recanted, he was likely uncomfortable with the direction of the national Democratic Party on issues of race and, of course as we saw in his 2004 RNC speech, matters of national security. In reality, Democrats moved decisively away from Miller's core principles in the 1970s and 1980s, and it was probably only the success of the New Democrats in the late 1980s that convinced him to stay in the fold. By the early 2000s, like a lot of members of the Silent Generation, Miller would sing a tune that goes something like, "I didn't leave the Democratic Party, the Democratic Party left me."

I focus on Miller not because he's a particularly odious figure—he did some good as the governor of Georgia, and I'd trade him straight up for Donald Trump without even thinking about it. Instead, Miller highlights how unusual, and perhaps unique, the transformation of the Silent Generation really was. The way that Democrats bled out with this group starting in the mid-1990s was almost entirely a function of New Deal liberals growing increasingly uncomfortable with the prominent role that racial minorities and women were beginning to play in party politics, and the way that the Democrat Party had seemed to move away from its Cold War–era hawkishness. In other words, members of the Silent Generation did not undergo mass ideological conversion—a certain number of them simply switched parties. The aftermath of 9/11 seems to loom particularly large here. Republicans took their first party ID lead with this generation in 2003 (only to surrender it due to the manifest disaster of Bush's second term). And it was the rise of Barack Obama, the first black president of the United States, that finally flipped them to Team Red for good. Many New Democrats stayed in the fold, and still represent the right flank of the party today; many others, like Miller, decamped to the GOP, and it seems like a substantial percentage of the Silent Generation followed.

Yet it is important to remember how unusual this story is. The defection of the Silent Generation from the Democratic Party was the function largely of one of the two political parties finally making good on the promises of emancipation for African Americans. The realignment of the South away from the Democratic Party beginning in the 1960s was, in many ways, a once-in-history kind of event, and the change in voting preferences of the Silent Generation have not been replicated in any other demographic-generation group since then. We also must remember that while there has been a massive shift in Silent Generation party ID, the voting patterns of this group have always been all over the place. Check out the Democratic and Republican vote share of people born between 1927 and 1942 as reported to researchers with the American National Election Study (ANES):[22]

	D	R
1948	70	30
1952	43	57
1956	42	58
1960	51	49
1964	70	30
1968	50	50
1972	35	65
1976	47	53
1980	38	62
1984	40	60
1988	49	51
1992	56	44
1996	56	44
2000	48	52
2004	51	49
2008	41	59
2012	44	56
2016	41	59

Boy howdy, I just don't know what to tell you here. Silents went 70–30 for Harry Truman in the first presidential election in which any of them were old enough to vote and then Eisenhower by double digits, and Johnson by forty points over Goldwater, and Nixon by thirty points over McGovern, and then Reagan by landslides, Clinton decisively, Bush, Kerry (!), and then McCain, Romney, and Trump. Overall, this group has voted for the Democrat in just six of eighteen presidential elections. I think it's fair to look at the overall trajectory of Silent politics and characterize them as quite a conservative generation, even if sometimes they voted for Democrats. This is a picture of a cohort of people who came of age in an era when the parties themselves weren't that different, when their economic policies (generally somewhat liberal) and their racial policies (united in protecting apartheid in the American South and mostly hostile to anything other than cosmetic justice initiatives) were similar enough that bouncing around between one party or the other between national elections didn't seem like quite as crazy a proposition as it might today. And with those voting patterns in mind, it makes a lot more sense that their party ID has made such a dramatic move since the early 1990s to the Republican Party.

It's not just the Silent Generation either. Despite their reputation as a large group of acid-dropping, long-haired radicals, most members of the baby boomer generation were also not especially liberal when they were young. While early boomers voted for Johnson in droves, giving him the same

70 percent of the vote Silents did, they also voted narrowly for Nixon twice, decisively for Reagan in 1980 and 1984, and then George H. W. Bush in 1988.[23] Members of this group gave the Democrat the same percentage of the vote in 1968 (49 percent) as they did in 2016 (48 percent). The members of Students for a Democratic Society may have gotten all the press attention, and Hollywood may want you to remember boomers exclusively through the lens of the antiwar movement, but it looks like most of them were much more ordinary when they were young—and that they basically never changed. For every David Horowitz, there were many more people who either started out as hippies and remained so forever or who began their political lives as conservative-leaning and never changed. Of course, there are differences inside the long boomer generation, but overall they are not nearly as liberal as the media stereotypes would have you believe.

Of course, some humbleness is in order here too. It is worth noting that the whole field of polling was born and matured in the lifetimes of the oldest members of the Silent Generation. Scientific public opinion research dates only to the 1930s. The realignment of American politics that began with the passage of civil rights legislation is less than sixty years old. It is certainly possible that unforeseen changes in the political system could soften partisanship in ways we cannot currently foresee. It is also plausible that events whose nature and impact we can scarcely imagine today might alter the preferences and beliefs of millennials and Gen

Zers—plagues, natural disasters, and other climate-related catastrophes could, rather than reinforce these generations' inclinations to fight back, instead lead to a scarcity-based politics of selfishness. Or the next Democratic government could prove to be such a policy disaster that the next set of incoming generations leans Republican. More on that in the conclusion. But for now, we can be reasonably confident that this long generation of leftists, beginning with younger Xers and stretching into the foreseeable future, will not only remain heavily Democratic, but that they will pass that partisanship on to their children. The future from that standpoint looks heavily Democratic.

But why?

CHAPTER 4

THE KIDS ARE A NIGHTMARE FOR THE GOP

EACH TRANSIENT POLITICAL triumph of our lifetimes has involved some seemingly critical group of swing voters, who are issued a catchy moniker by political reporters. In the '80s it was Reagan Democrats, former liberals who were more or less permanently transformed by the rise of Ronald Reagan. In the early 2000s it was the so-called "soccer moms" or "security moms" who voted for Bush and the Republicans. In each case, the key to victory for one party or the other was alleged to be some discrete sliver of the electorate that flipped in between electoral cycles. For the Republicans today, this is the much-discussed "Obama-Trump voter," those who cast their ballots for Barack Obama in 2012 but Donald Trump in 2016. The Democratic capture of the House of Representatives in 2018 was dependent in some particularly competitive districts on winning some of these Obama-Trump voters back.

The coming realignment of American politics I envision

in this book doesn't depend on soccer dads or Trump Democrats. If current demographic trends hold, national elections will seldom be decided by some sexy microgroup of voters who seem to gravitate en masse from one party to another between elections. It is grounded in a great, multifaceted generational transformation, one that is slowly but ineluctably shrinking the country's white population and growing its share of nonwhites. It is related to an ongoing national decline in religiosity and the gradual but discernible increases in share of Americans getting a college degree. This transformation shows no particular signs of being influenced by temporary political reversals or events. And young people are its driver.

In chapter 2, I explained how the nearly twenty-year trend in younger voters supporting Democrats is a massive departure from the political past, even the recent past. And in chapter 3, I explained why nothing is likely to shake a significant percentage of these young Democrats loose from their partisanship. But it is one thing to identify some empirical trend. It is quite another to explain it. Though the implications are poorly understood by analysts and observers, I should hope by now that it is indisputable that young people have been voting sharply Democratic since the early 2000s, and that the original cohorts of lefty youth have now thoroughly conquered the thirty-to-forty-four voting demographic and tilted it decisively toward Team Blue.

Let's recap for a second before plunging you into more data. America is deeply polarized and has been characterized by very close presidential and congressional elections for thirty years—the entire political consciousness of probably half of the Americans alive today. But since the turn of this new century, the emergence of a center-left majority has been prevented only by a combination of US institutional design oddities like the Electoral College and deliberate Republican rat-fucking at every single level of government, perpetrated in general by the ten worst human beings in every graduating class. Our close divisions have only made us hate one another more, and that emotionally driven polarization has been accompanied by the slow drift of the parties away from one another ideologically. Yet underneath this placid surface of stalemate, a tsunami is building which could reorient American politics for decades—the steady leftward movement of the country's youngest voters, and the emergence of a now-thirty-year-long bloc of heavily Democratic voters. Political science suggests that the voting patterns, ideological beliefs and partisan attachments of voters are set in early adulthood, and there is little hope for Republicans to stage a comeback with these same people twenty or thirty years from now. The idea that young liberals turn into old conservatives is an anecdote-driven myth. And unless the GOP turns around its fortunes with the next few cohorts of incoming eighteen-year-old voters or tears democracy down in an effort to prevent the inevitable, Republicans are good and screwed.

This all leaves us, though, with the question of why. What has moved young voters to the left so decisively? The answer is a complicated mix. It involves both massive demographic and behavioral transformation as well as what are the increasingly plain and negative consequences of Republican policy-making and cultural attitudes. The good news for Republicans is that they could probably arrest their losses with new voting cohorts if the party could find the will to change. The bad news is that the country's demographic shift is permanent and irreversible without the commission of war crimes against America's own citizens. In other words, some of this is already well out of the hands of Republican elites. But let's start with policy.

While casual observers of politics tend to overestimate the importance particular policies to voters, that doesn't mean that the stances of political parties on major national issues are meaningless. In *The Great Alignment*, Alan Abramowitz argued that, over time, individuals have sorted themselves into the political party that best fits their underlying beliefs, and that Democrats agree with other Democrats across a wide variety of issue areas, including racial justice, the role of the state in the national economy, and more. Likewise for Republicans. If you are pro-life, you are also now overwhelmingly likely to express support for tax cuts and deregulation and opposition to gun control measures. These sets of issues bear no intrinsic ideological relationship to one another—some are cultural, and some are related to the size and scope of the social welfare state. But as Abramowitz notes, the attitudes of Democrats and Republicans on these disparate issues are statistically correlated much more so than in the past. "It is clear that opinions on these types of issues are increasingly likely to reinforce one another," he writes.[1] Some of this could be related to geographic sorting, and some of it could simply be the influence of party elites on mass opinion. Whatever the case, there aren't many pro-life, pro-gun, anti-tax Democrats left in the party's big tent, and there are precious few pro-immigration, pro–Medicare for All, anti–second amendment voters left in the Republican fold.

Millennials and Zers were born into the hyperpartisan world forged by their parents and grandparents. And for the most part, they are choosing to identify with and vote for the party that best represents their policy preferences. For sure, as was discussed in chapter 3, they may have largely inherited those preferences from their parents, but in a highly polarized and closely divided electorate, and in a world in which members of these generations are mostly dating, marrying, socializing with, and living near copartisans, both by choice and by geographic necessity, we should not be surprised to see young people fitting policy desires and party loyalty together neatly. More importantly, the two-party system on offer to these young Americans is characterized by wild differences on important matters of public policy. While you still get the stray malcontent claiming that Democrats and Republicans are indistinguishable—"tweedle dee" and "tweedle dum"—it is a much more difficult argument to make persuasively in today's climate. Voters can feel the dramatic ideological difference between someone like Paul Ryan, who favors rolling the size of American government back to what it was in the nineteenth century, and Bernie Sanders, who wants an enormous expansion of the states' roles in the economy and in society.

Particularly once they get out of the house and into college or their first jobs, young voters have their first opportunity to look at the political world without the influence of their parents. And what these young Americans have been telling pollsters, for a very long time now, is that on nearly all pertinent issues of American public policy, they either agree with Democrats by very wide margins, or they are to the left of both parties. This goes for economic issues, like the health-care system, foreign policy issues like American interventionism, and cultural issues like abortion and same-sex marriage. Millennials and Zers are, by orders of magnitude, the most left-wing generations ever.

This has been true since survey organizations started compiling data about millennials. In the 2008 exit polls—the first ones in which almost everyone in the eighteen-to-twenty-nine age group was a Pew-defined "millennial"—the youngest voters expressed startlingly left-wing positions on significant issues. Sixty-nine percent said that "the government should do more to solve problems," as opposed to just 41 percent of those sixty-five years and older. Nearly twice as many young voters described themselves as "liberal" than the oldest voters.[2] But the realization that millennials were profoundly liberal only started to happen in 2009. In December of that year, Pew began releasing reports with the moniker, "Millennials: A Portrait of Generation Next." The first was about interracial marriage and found that 93 percent of millennials approved, as opposed to just 68 percent of Silents.[3] Other reports found that millennials were much less likely than their elders to express mindless patriotic sentiment, with a 2013 report finding that just 32 percent of millennials think that America is the greatest country in the world, as opposed to half of boomers and 61 percent of Silents.[4]

There are blizzards of data out there to bore you with, but suffice it to say that over the years, millennials (and later, Zers) were found to have more progressive stances on a variety of issues. I went through the Harvard Youth Poll's spring survey back to 2006 and looked at topline data for four representative issues.[5] One asks whether health insurance is a basic right and if the government should provide it for those who can't afford it. Another asks whether homosexual relationships (later worded as "same-sex relationships") are morally wrong. A third asks whether it is sometimes necessary to attack hostile countries before they attack us first. And the fourth asks whether cutting taxes is the best way to spur economic growth. I've combined the percentage who agree and somewhat agree in the chart below.

	BASIC HEALTH INSURANCE RIGHT	HOMOSEXUAL RELATIONSHIPS WRONG	NECESSARY TO ATTACK	CUTTING TAXES
2006	73	26	25	21
2007	61	27	28	32
2008	61	30	27	37
2010	47	29	24	41
2011	49	25	20	39
2012	44	25	22	39
2013	42	27	25	41
2016	48	26	23	35
2017	46	25	21	33
2019	52	22	24	36

The data here is quite consistent, with most questions bouncing around in ways that don't seem significant in any way. Eighteen-to-twenty-nine-year-olds since 2006 have been anti-interventionist in foreign policy, opposed to tax cuts as economic policy, and opposed to discrimination against LGBTQI citizens. The only issue here where we see significant change is on health insurance, with young Americans first expressing strong support for the idea of insurance as a right, only to see that number plummet to 42 percent during the Obama Administration and rebound to 52 percent in the most recent poll. Some of this fluctuation surely reflects frustration with the botched rollout of the Affordable Care Act in 2013, as well as the overall harshly negative national climate related to the ACA between its passage and the 2016 election.

It is also worth noting that in the spring of 2019, 55 percent of eighteen-to-twenty-nine-year-olds supported a single-payer health-care system. And just to reiterate, the oldest survey respondents from 2006 are now forty-three years old. The 2006 survey and the 2019 survey include no cohort overlap. These are different sets of people with essentially the same views on government interventionism, culture war problems, and foreign policy. I've combed through this data multiple times, and you'd be hard-pressed to find responses to any question that consistently fit with the positions of the contemporary Republican Party. It's remarkable.

At the same time, survey data consistently found that they were worse off economically than prior generations— more likely to live at home (36 percent of eighteen-to-thirty-one-year-olds in 2013 as compared to 32 percent in 1968, with a big increase in people "living with kin" on top),[6] significantly less likely to own a home (35 percent of those under thirty-five owned their own home in 2013, compared with more than 43 percent in 2004),[7] and often saddled with student debt, whether or not they finished a degree. In 2014, college-educated young adults who took out loans to pay for their education had a debt load that was on average 206 percent of their household income—almost double the rate from 2001.[8] The average age of first-time home-buyers reached its highest point in the post-WWII period—thirty-three years old, up from thirty in 2007.[9] The percentage of millennials considered middle class is just 60 percent, down from 70 percent of boomers.[10] In 2001, 55 percent of those under the age of thirty-five owned stock. By 2018, it was 37 percent. As *The Atlantic*'s Annie Lowrey put it, "The net worth of your average millennial household is 40 percent lower than for Gen X households in 2001 and 20 percent lower than for Baby Boomers' households at the end of the 1980s."[11]

And on and on and on. It would be difficult to find any metric by which millennials are better off economically than members of previous generations. And there's little chance that they will ever make up the ground lost in the Great Recession and due to the dreadful economic policies of this century. While we might expect Generation Z to be in a somewhat better starting position as they embark on their adult lives, they will also be dealing with the same structural factors that have hampered the millennials: soaring costs for health care, higher education, and housing. Particularly in the top tier cities like San Francisco, Washington, DC, Boston, Los Angeles, Chicago, and New York, housing costs eat up an incredible share of earnings, even for young people who make good salaries and don't have outstanding debt loads. And God only knows what the COVID-19 crisis, which may spike unemployment to Great Depression levels or worse, could do to the generation now emerging onto the job market.

It is no mystery who is taking the blame for this economic mess: the Republican Party. The GOP is not just on the wrong side of cultural issues like abortion and same-sex marriage. It is on the wrong side of millennial and Z economic interests. And it is on the wrong side of the issue that is likely to define politics for Zers throughout their lives: climate change. In survey after survey, young respondents express greater concern about climate change and favor more active measures to combat it, as compared with older generations. In American politics, with only two major parties, you don't need voters to agree with you on every single issue, or even most issues, to get them to support you. Sometimes voters will make their decisions based on one thing—the fabled single-issue voters. But voters do need to agree with you about *something*. And the GOP has systematically positioned itself far outside the public opinion mainstream on almost every conceivable issue that young people might care about. For God's sake, the official position of the national Republican Party is still that marijuana use should be prohibited altogether. In one 2019 poll, 85 percent of eighteen-to-thirty-four-year-olds supported marijuana legalization.[12] It is just insanity to oppose something that has 85 percent support among voters.

That's today's Republican Party. Gripped by a relentless will to political suicide. But there is something even more important driving millennial and Gen Z repulsion from the Republican Party—the changing nature of race, education, and religion in the United States.

Cold truth: there is not a single demographic factor in the millennial and Z generations that benefits the Republican Party. Let's start with whiteness. While the political press has made a huge deal out of Hillary Clinton's losses with white voters in 2016, Democrats have been losing the white vote forever with no end in sight. Bill Clinton's achievement of nabbing 44 percent of white voters in the 1996 election was the party's post-realignment high. Obama got 39 percent of the white vote in 2012 and still managed to win reelection. The Republican Party's sharp but not overwhelming advantage with white voters, together with the heavily white composition of the Silent and boomer generations has allowed it to weather staggering disadvantages with voters of color.

THE RACIAL AND ETHNIC MAKEUP OF AMERICA'S GENERATIONS

% of 6- to 21-year olds who are...

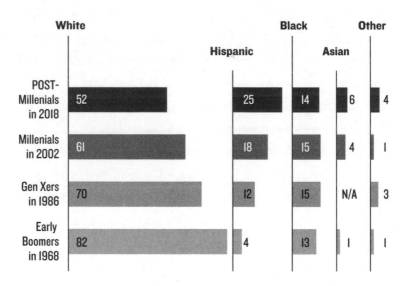

Note: Racial groups include only single-race non Hispanics. Hispanics are of any race. Asians include Pacific Islanders. The CPS did not separately identify Asians until 1988. Hispanic origin was not collected until 1971. The racial and ethnic composition of Boomers in 1968 was imputed on the basis of 8- to 23-year olds in the 1970 census.
Source: Pew Research Center analysis of 1968, 2002 and 2018 Current Population Survey Annual Social and Economic Supplements and 1970 decennial census (IPUMS). 'Early Benchmarks Show Post-Millennial on Track to Be Most Diverse, Best-Educated Generation Yet', PEW RESEARCH CENTER

Why do people of color vote Democratic in such huge numbers? Let's start with the most decisively Democratic group in the country. On average, 88 percent of African Americans have voted Democratic in presidential and congressional elections dating back to 1980. As such, they represent the most lopsided voting bloc in American politics and provide the margin of victory for the Democratic Party in nearly every successful federal election. It is not immediately obvious why this should be so, since African Americans are not ideologically homogeneous and on average are more conservative than the white progressives who tend to drive left political discourse online. And it turns out that the answer is somewhat contested in the scholarship. Many political scientists accept a version of the "Black Utility Heuristic," first posed by Michael Dawson in 1994. In *Behind the Mule: Race and Class in African American Politics*, Dawson proposed that the unique circumstances of black Americans forces them to consider the effect of individual votes on the group as a whole.[13] Your fate is linked to the black community as a whole, and so voters tend to cast ballots for candidates of the party presumed to be better for black interests.

Dawson, fascinatingly, mused about the era that we are currently living through, and its potential impact on black politics. "What if the economic environment improved," he asked, "but the racial environment deteriorated?" It is hard to know how else to describe the first three years of the Trump era. The president constantly brags about record-low black unemployment, a data point relentlessly parroted by his apologists in the media. Yet President Trump has also ushered in a period of renewed and ugly divisions between white and black America. From his endless feuding on Twitter with black politicians like Maxine Waters and John Lewis to his unglued ranting about NFL players kneeling to protest police violence against African Americans (and indeed, his fetishization and encouragement of that brutality), Trump's rhetoric exceeds even Reagan's dog-whistling about "welfare queens" and the early-1990s panic about "superpredators" in the annals of post–World War II official racism. Dawson predicted that a Trumplike era would see "serious conflict over strategies and tactics within the black community," although he stopped short of saying that the African American vote would be more evenly divided between the parties under such circumstances.[14]

So far the long economic expansion that Trump goosed by finally unleashing government spending that Republicans held hostage under Obama has failed to move black voters away from support for the Democratic Party. According to network exit polls, African Americans voted Democratic in House and Senate races by 81 points, 90 percent to 9 percent. There is no better news as you drill down into these exit polls. Black voters aged eighteen to twenty-nine voted Democratic 92–7, an 8-point swing from the oldest voters. Thirty-to-forty-four-year-old black voters, mostly older millennials, voted blue by the same 85-point margin. You can't place this all at the feet of Trump, but record-high numbers of African Americans now say that "racism is a big problem in society today."[15] Whether it is depressing regularity of innocent men and women gunned down by trigger-happy cops, an administration staffed almost entirely by white guys, or perhaps even the racial wealth gap that has barely budged even during these good times, the African American community in the United States is not reacting to the economy the way that other groups are. The only good tidings for the GOP in any of this data is that the black electorate as a whole is not growing as compared to the white share.

The same can't be said for the Latinx and Asian electorate. Whites have gone from 82 percent of young boomers in 1968 to just 52 percent of young Zers in 2018. The cause of this sudden demographic shift, which has caused so much vitriolic racism on the American right, is patterns of immigration from Latin America to the United States since the 1960s. Between 1965 and 2016, 16 million people immigrated to the United States from Mexico, an enormously consequential migration pattern that has increased the Hispanic[16] share of the American population from 3.5 percent in 1960 to about 18 percent today. While Mexican immigration has stalled out, arrivals from other countries in Latin America, particularly the troubled states of Central America like Honduras and Guatemala, have shot up. Unfortunately for the Stephen Millers of the world and all of his fellow nativists, immigration itself is no longer the primary force propelling the Latinx share of the population upward. In the 1980s, immigration added 5.6 million people to the Latinx population, and births in the United States added 4.4. The numbers were similar, but higher in the 1990s, when immigration added 8.1 million. Yet between 2010 and 2015, births in America were responsible for nearly three times the growth in the Latinx population as immigration itself.[17] The growth of the Latinx population in the United States is expected to continue indefinitely, with the Latinx share of the overall population reaching more than 28 percent by 2060.[18] Draconian crackdowns and deportations might be able to dent these numbers but are unlikely to substantially change America's demographic future. It is baked in.

And as the percentage of Hispanics and Asians (a combined 5 percent in 1968 to a combined 31 percent in 2018) has skyrocketed, and as both groups vote roughly 2–1 Democratic, the GOP's fortunes with young people have collapsed accordingly. Those losses have not been offset by any meaningful gains with young whites.

Despite recognizing in its post-2012 autopsy that appealing to Latinx voters was a critical need for the GOP, subsequent elected Republicans failed to change their policy positions or to reach out in any meaningful way to younger Latinx voters. Here again, you can see the Republican position slipping badly with the youngest members of the group. Latinx aged sixty-five and older voted Democratic in 2018 by a 71–25 margin, yet eighteen-to-twenty-nine-year-olds swung 18 points more blue, 81–17. Millennial Latinx voted 18 points more Democratic than those aged forty-five to sixty-four. Republicans have, therefore, traded their long-term viability with incoming generations for fleeting viability with people who might soon die. This is certainly understandable from a short-term strategic standpoint, but incomprehensible for the long duree.

A recent study by Monica Escaleras, Dukhong Kim, and Kevin Wagner suggests that Latinx too vote based on perceptions of shared fate and group interest.[19] They created an original survey of Latinx voters in the 2014 midterms and the 2016 presidential election. They included a statement that addressed the question of linked fates: "What happens generally to other Latinos/Hispanics in this country affects what happens in your life." Respondents who said yes to this statement were much more likely to vote Democratic in both elections. Critically, the percent who responded positively to the shared destiny question increased more than 10 points between the 2014 and 2016 elections, almost certainly due to the vitriolic racist rhetoric spewing like an oil geyser from the mouth of the Republican nominee. The GOP's recent rightward turn on immigration matters only increases the likelihood that Latinx voters will continue to vote Democratic by overwhelming margins. However, there is significant evidence to suggest that, as Alan Yang and Rodolfo de la Garza argue, Latinx are "a distinct segment of the electorate characterized primarily by an almost unanimous support for a government-supported social-safety net." As such, Latinx are likely to continue leaning Democratic "even were the Republican Party to moderate its position on immigration."[20]

Insofar as Latinx do vote Republican, demography is still not working in the GOP's favor. The most heavily Republican Latinx group, Cuban exiles in Florida, is rapidly aging. Florida's Cuban voters went for Trump in 2016 by a 54–41 margin. Yet age-related decline and the absence of fresh waves of Cuban immigrants has diminished the salience of Cuban voters even in Florida, where they now constitute just 31 percent of the Latinx population.[21] And because partisanship works its magic on Latinx just as much as it does on whites, if younger Latinx lean Democratic by roughly the 3–1 margin we saw in 2018, then the next generation of Latinx voters is likely to be overwhelmingly Democratic just based on the dynamics of inherited partisanship.

President Trump is doing everything in his power to make the Republican deficit with Latinx voters worse. His racist obsession with undocumented immigrants needs no recitation here. From his creation of a government database to track victims of crime by undocumented immigrants to his decision to rescind protections under Obama's Deferred Action for Childhood Arrivals (DACA) program to the administration's incredibly cruel and borderline genocidal policy of separating small children from parents at the US-Mexico border, the Trump presidency has been a long and relentless attack on Latinx immigrants. In polling by the firm Latino Decisions, the number of Latinx who say that "racism against Latinos and immigrants" is a "major problem" spiked from 51 percent to 62 percent just over the course of 2019 alone.[22]

While Republicans maintain much stronger support among the Latinx electorate than they have in the African American electorate, the consequences of losing a particular population by 2–1 margins grow more dire as that population grows. It's one thing to lose a voter pool of a million people 670,000 to 330,000. It's quite another to lose a voting pool of forty million people by that same margin.

There is worse news for Republicans and Generation Z: this cohort is more likely to tell pollsters that they intend to pursue a college education than past generations and are much more likely to live with a college-educated parent. In 2002, just under a third of millennials lived with a college-educated parent. For Zers in 2018, that number was 43 percent. Of course, not everyone who pursues a college degree gets one—53 percent of millennials in 2002 said they wanted to go to college, but only about 39 percent have gotten a degree. Yet this figure represents a massive increase in the college-educated population over previous generations. At a comparable point in their generation evolution, only 29 percent of Gen Xers had a college degree, about a quarter of boomers, and just 15 percent among those in the Silent Generation.[23] If the attrition rate for Gen Z is the same as it was for millennials, as many as 45 percent may get their bachelor's degree. This is a much more significant development than it might seem because of the increasing education gap in

American elections, with college-educated people of all races and backgrounds voting much more heavily Democratic over time. In 1992, Americans with at least a BA identified as or leaned toward Republicans 49–45. Today that group prefers Democrats by 22 points, 58–36. Americans without a college degree have gone from 55–36 Democratic to 47–45 Republican. That narrow edge among the non-college-educated is not enough, today, to offset the GOP's losses among the credentialed. As the highly educated, highly diverse Generation Z's share of the electorate starts to creep up beginning with the 2020 election, Republicans will have a hard time maintaining their power unless they make further inroads with other demographic groups.

Young people are also moving away from the Republican Party because they are becoming much less religious than older generations, and the Republican Party has yoked itself ever more closely to hardline evangelism. The youths are not feeling God, at least not in the way that their elders once did. Younger Americans are leaving the rural and exurban areas where religion is the strongest and moving to diverse cities and suburbs where it is weird to yell out "Jesus Christ!" earnestly.

For millennials, there has been a 16-point drop in self-identified Christians just since 2009, with a 13-point increase in those who say they are "unaffiliated."[24] About 35 percent of millennials identify as atheist, agnostic, or nothing in particular, an extraordinary increase from these numbers among boomers and Silents. Just 11 percent of the latter and 17 percent of the former fit themselves into this category in 2014. The data we have on Generation Z suggests that the numbers for incoming voters are quite similar. Americans aged thirteen to eighteen in 2018 identified as atheists at more than twice the rate of the general population, and just 59 percent described themselves as Christian. Fifty-nine percent said that "Church is not relevant to me personally."[25] It should be particularly worrisome that a significant subset of self-identifying Christians think the Church itself is not important to them.

Others may retain their faith but leave evangelical circles due to the off-putting nature of the church's alliance with the immoral dumpster goblins of the Trump era, or perhaps because people who really believe in God would prefer that human beings not turn his creation into an uninhabitable steam room whose oceans are acidified graveyards. Like millennials, Gen Zers also have a hard time squaring the existence of God with the amount of suffering currently happening in the world. But probably the most important factor is that their parents are less religious than their grandparents, and therefore they are less likely to be pious given their home backgrounds. This is trouble for Republicans because Protestants, and white evangelicals in particular, provided the margin for Donald Trump's victory in 2016—Protestants overall voted for him by 17 points. Shave a point or two off of those margins in the key states of Michigan, Wisconsin, and

Pennsylvania via elderly evangelicals dying and not getting replaced with younger ones, and Trump's chances this year as well as the Republican path to victory become much murkier.

The most religious Americans have been critical to Republican power for generations now, and the tight alliance between evangelical Christians and the GOP is more important than ever. It wasn't always so—as recently as the 1948 presidential election, just 38 percent of US evangelicals voted for the Republican presidential candidate, Thomas Dewey.[26] Yet during the Cold War, an ever-closer alliance between Republicans and white evangelicals gradually developed, based on anti-communism as well as hostility to some of the decisions of the Warren Court, especially *Roe v. Wade*. Led by Billy Graham, born-again Christians grew in political strength and importance, leveraging a network of right-wing organizations for fund-raising and election day turnout to become an important force in American politics. By the time Ronald Reagan was elected in 1980, these voters were a core constituency of the Republican Party and have remained so ever since. Yet depending on highly religious white voters as a strategy is already running into limitations. To begin with, Republicans have won the national popular vote for the presidency just once since 1988, a sharp reversal from the 1968–88 period, when Democrats won just a single presidential election in 1976, driven more by the GOP's post-Watergate hangover than by any real, sustained success with the electorate.

Of course, discussions of religion in US politics need to

be disambiguated. Some religious groups, including Jews and Muslims, vote heavily Democratic. Protestants have long voted heavily Republican, but in 2016, Donald Trump won the Catholic vote by 7 points, a reversal from recent elections this century. The Democratic advantage with Jews held steady, with Hillary Clinton performing better than Barack Obama in 2012, although not as well as Al Gore in 2000, John Kerry in 2004, or Obama in 2008. Ultimately the most important factor leading Republicans to win religious Americans over-all is the party's overwhelming edge with white evangelical Christians. Donald Trump won 81 percent of those voters in 2016, and all indications are that he has preserved this sup-port, despite his lifelong record of greed, adultery, and grift. George W. Bush won these voters 78–21 in 2004.[27]

But the news about the future of this evangelical vote is not great for Republicans either. In the 2018 General Social Sur-vey, for instance, those expressing no affiliation outnumbered evangelicals for the first time, 23.1 percent to 22.5 percent.[28] The "white evangelical" share of the population dropped from 17 percent in 2016 to 15.3 percent in 2018.[29] That overall decrease has been masked in recent years by the unusually high turnout for white evangelicals in national America elec-tions. But turnout gains cannot cover up the loss of adherents forever. Indeed, as the more diverse and less religious Gen-eration Z matures into political power, the white evangelical share of the US population is likely to drop precipitously and take Republicans fortunes with it unless the party can either make substantial inroads with other religious groups or dent the Democrats' advantage with nonaffiliated voters.

Remember: it is not enough for Republicans to simply stop the bleeding on these trends. They have to be reversed, and quickly. Just as our theoretical baseball commissioner needs to increase youth interest in the game rather than simply end the losses, it is not enough for Republicans to arrest the party's decline with younger voters. At some point they have to start winning them, or at least not getting crushed. That means expanding the party's advantage with white voters, or cutting into the Democrats' advantage with voters of color, nonreligious Americans, and women.

But hang on a second. What about Charlie Kirk and Tomi Lahren and all those aggressive, young white conservatives you see every night on *Fox News*? Aren't these in-your-face, Trumpified young conservatives gaining traction and importance in our national politics? And might they not at some point have enough strength and credibility to challenge their more liberal generational counterparts?

I mean, read on, but no.

CHAPTER 5

SOME OF THE KIDS ARE CONSERVATIVES

ON MAY 13, 2018, a young woman named Kaitlin Bennett tweeted a picture of herself after her graduation from Kent State University. In the picture, Bennett was toward the right of the frame, facing away from the camera with an AR-15 strapped to her back, the muzzle pointed down and to the right. In her right hand, the top of her black graduation cap read "Come and take it," with a white rifle painted in the middle. The tweet read, "Now that I graduated from @KentState, I can finally arm myself on campus. I should have been able to do so as a student—especially since four unarmed students were shot and killed by the government on this campus," and was hashtagged #CampusCarryNow. It was retweeted more than 8,000 times and received more than 35,000 likes, and it earned her the sobriquet "Gun Girl." The sort of celebrity whose meteoric and confounding rise to fame could only happen in the social media era, Bennett now has more than 228,000 followers on Twitter and operates her own website, which is called Liberty Hangout, and seems designed to show visitors as many racy pictures of Bennett holding guns as possible.

Liberty Hangout does not look or feel like a venture designed for longtime success, but Bennett is representative of a new species of young conservative—brash, telegenic, and intoxicated on the dizzying combination of hyperpartisanship and grifter-doofus scamming that characterizes the thought leaders of the young right. Bennett was the leader of Kent State's chapter of Turning Points USA, which made national headlines when it had a student dress up in a diaper and pacifier to mock the proliferation of safe spaces on campus. TPUSA is an organization founded by the similarly absurd young conservative Charlie Kirk to fight left-wing radicalism on campuses across the country. Like Bennett, Kirk has a very simple grift—do and say genuinely outrageous things, capture campus leftists reacting badly to those things on video, disseminate the video, and then let the likes, clicks, and donations roll in.

Kirk, a fixture on *Fox News* outrage roundtables, is a hyperaggressive shill whose mind-numbing toadyism for President Trump is impressive if nothing else than for the sheer scale and dedication of its obsequiousness. Kirk is the author of *Campus Battlefield: How Conservatives Can WIN the Battle on Campus and Why It Matters*, a book that prominently features many of Kirk's own tweets sandwiched around galaxy-sized swaths of blank space.[1]

Kirk's role as national conservative campus provocateur is especially peculiar considering that he never went to college (he was reportedly rejected from West Point) and crafts prose that would immediately get flagged as remedial in any introductory college writing seminar: "If America is so bad," he asks, "why do so many people want in? Millions are so anxious to come to America that they are literally climbing over fences, swimming rivers, and figuratively busting down doors."[2] How does one figuratively bust down a door, you might ask? If someone wants to get into America, presumably they must do things literally rather than figuratively.

Kirk's brand of conservatism is clearly ascendant on the right, part of a kind of Clod Squad featuring writers like Ben Shapiro (*The Right Side of History: How Reason and Moral Purpose Made the West Great*) and Candace Owens (*Blackout: How Black America Can Make Its Second Escape from the Democrat Plantation*). Together they represent a sharp departure from the young conservatism of yore. While these writers differ in depth and quality (Shapiro is a convincingly read, Harvard-trained lawyer, whereas Owens is a college dropout spouting nonsense about the "Democrat plantation"), they do share a certain aesthetic. When I was in college, the young Republicans were cardigan-wearing bookworms, well-read if misguided nerds, more likely to dress up as William F. Buckley than as diaper-clad babies, and more interested in writing for the campus conservative rag or running for student government than staging media stunts designed to catapult them into instafame. Today's prominent young conservative activists either eschew college altogether, attend solely for the purpose of getting very angry and defensive with the liberals and progressives they think surround them at all times or go to Liberty University or Hillsdale College, where the comprehensive lack of evidence for anything they believe in will produce less cognitive dissonance.

The movement traffics in arguments that are prima facie absurd. For instance, following the lead of the genuinely absurd Dinesh D'Souza, younger Republicans like Owen openly advance the argument that today's Democrats are the party of slavery, because that's what the nineteenth-century Democratic Party was. Or as he himself put it, "If the progressives didn't cover for Democrats, they'd have to explain why they are in the very same party that enslaved blacks, segregated them, lynched them and has to this day refused to admit this, to officially apologize or to pay one penny in restitution for its crimes."[3] Four weeks or so of an introductory American history seminar should be enough to disabuse anyone of the idea that today's Democrats, now unquestionably the party of minority rights and African American political power, are somehow responsible for the sins of slavery or that they alone should bear the cost of restitution. D'Souza knows that Republicans and Democrats switched sides in the fight for civil rights in the 1950s and 1960s, and that the Republican Party soon became the institutional home of people continuing the fight to deny equal rights to the descendants of slaves. He's not stupid—like many in the Trumpified political right today, what he is doing is testing his movement's boundaries of credulity, to demonstrate the power and reach of naked propaganda and transparently ludicrous arguments. And he has found enthusiastic young backers for this effort in people like Kirk, Owens, and Lahren.

These young conservatives are united by a kind of permanent sense of aggrievement, the belief that the United States is culturally dominated by liberals and progressives and that conservatives are some sort of oppressed class. "Liberals are unafraid to put their political views out there," writes Tomi Lahren, "because they have this indulgent, conceited idea that they always have the moral high ground."[4] Like their elders, these young conservatives (many of whom seem to not have finished college) are totally and weirdly obsessed with the goings-on at campuses they do not attend. In his book about the superiority of the West, *The Right Side of History*, Ben Shapiro devotes several pages of the introduction to sharing a tale of woe about how one of his speeches at Cal State Los Angeles got canceled. "I refused to accede to that clear breach of First Amendment rights," he thunders, "and I announced that I would show up anyway."[5] There were some protestors there, as you might imagine. Someone pulled the fire alarm during his talk. "I spoke through the discord," Shapiro maintains, as if he was leading a regiment through the Ardennes rather than relieving some campus organization of its student activity dollars in exchange for an evening of cheap thrills. As protestors continued to dog him throughout his various publicity tours, Shapiro concluded: "We've lost something."[6] Mind you, this is the frame that he chooses before presenting the reader with a tour of "thousands of years of philosophy and history."

In fact, staged provocations at campuses around the country has been part of the conservative celebrity grift since the 1990s, a circuit trailblazed by people like the bomb-thrower Ann Coulter and the former leftist turned provocateur David Horowitz. Nonstop campus tours not only provide a hefty cut of the dough to keep movement thinkers employed, they supply a ready-made highlight reel of campus liberals saying outrageous things to speakers. The nexus between campus agitprop groups and conservative publishing was never clearer than when someone photographed hundreds of copies of Donald Trump Jr.'s book *Triggered* at a Turning Points USA chapter.

Shapiro is probably the most famous, and in the long run, the most consequential of these voices. Presumably the end of the Trump presidency will cut into the appeal of people like cable news gadfly Harlan Hill or Diamond & Silk. But Shapiro, who hosts one of the top-rated podcasts in the country, will likely be haunting you for the rest of your life in one capacity or another. If you've only listened to resistance podlandia staples like *Pod Save America, The Weeds,* or even hard-left shows like *Chapo Trap House,* I encourage you to give Shapiro's show a listen. You can almost hear his trademark scowl. He sounds always annoyed, and his terse, nasal delivery is the perfect vehicle for the standard-issue grievance politics that have dominated the conservative publishing and celebrity machine since the 1980s. Instead of ads for Stitch Fix and ZipRecruiter, Shapiro reads out bizarre ads for guns and investing in precious metals. In a run of episodes leading into 2020, Shapiro covered the "War on Christmas," interviewed Kirk Cameron, the former child TV star who went on to star in the evangelical *Left Behind* movies and is one of the recognizable conservatives in the business, and defend Harry Potter author J. K. Rowling from accusations of transphobia. And because he has positioned himself as an occasional critic of President Trump, his notoriety should survive past the president's term in office and grip on our public life.

Shapiro, who has pretensions to a kind of intellectual seriousness, founded the right-wing site *The Daily Wire*, and shares with people like Lahren, Bennett, and Kirk a kind of in-your-face attitude, an aesthetic designed to grow a social media following with aggressive posts and a calculated loathing of Democrats, liberals, progressives, Hollywood elites, professors, feminists, and other villains from the gallery. You might think of them as young Twitter conservatives.

If you watch *Fox News* or *The Blaze* or you read *Breitbart* and *The Federalist*, you could be forgiven for thinking that aggressive, in-your-face people like Bennett and Kirk are the future, or even that they are representative of their cohort. And while it is true that they have built up, quickly, a successful model of influencing and discourse-domination, thus far it has not been successful at bending the worldviews even of Gen Z Republicans, who from what little data we thus far have about them, are more liberal than even their millennial GOP peers. Similar to how we have come to understand that the political viewpoints of the most engaged Democrats on Twitter are not representative of either the broader population of Democrats or Americans in general, Kirkism doesn't seem like it represents how much young conservatives think or write or conceptualize their place in the world. For every hyped-up campus activist, there are many more young conservatives who live more or less ordinary lives, both in and out of college. Most young Republicans do what most young people do in college—they go to their classes and write their research papers and join nonpolitical clubs and party too much and study abroad. They do not turn out for events run by Turning Points USA, let alone participate in one of the group's ostentatious spectacles.

We have relatively limited data about the beliefs of young conservatives, but one significant batch of information comes from the Harvard Institute of Politics Youth Poll, conducted every two years and that talks exclusively to eighteen-to-twenty-nine-year-olds. Its most recent survey was published in the fall of 2019 and mostly conveyed unsurprising results.[7] Young people, for instance, care about climate change and believe that baby boomers don't care what happens to them. They skew Democratic. President Trump's approval rating with this group of more than two thousand respondents was

27 percent, with 71 percent disapproving. They disapprove of Trump's handling of the economy by nearly 20 points. These numbers all track closely with exit polling over the past few cycles which suggested that the youngest voters were continuing to move sharply leftward in their politics and ideology.

Overall, like any poll collected with data from this age cohort this century, it was not an encouraging set of results for Republicans. Digging into the crosstabs, however, makes it even worse. Obviously, the GOP's numbers look better with young Republicans than with everyone else. The president's approval is 74 percent with young Republicans. By 81–17, they approve of his handling of the economy. They approve of how he is handling health care by 40 points, 69–29. But those numbers are much lower than for Republicans overall. In Gallup's last poll of 2019, for example, Trump's approval with Republicans was 90 percent.[8] In a December 2019 Quinnipiac University poll, it was 92 percent.[9] The Trump drop-off with young Republicans is very real, and discernible in just about every question you ask them. According to the Harvard poll, 22 percent of young Republicans will "never" or are "unlikely" to vote to reelect President Trump. Just 64 percent say they are either sure or likely to vote for him.

The GOP's troubles with young Republicans appear to be issue-driven. According to another survey, this one conducted by Pew, 43 percent of Gen Z Republicans agree that "blacks aren't treated fairly," compared to just 30 percent of millennial GOPers and (brace yourself) 20 percent of boomer and Silent Generation Republicans. More than 52 percent of young Republicans "believe government should be doing more to solve problems" and only 18 percent were willing to endorse the crackpot theory that the earth is warming because of "natural patterns" rather than human activity. President Trump's dreadful job approval rating among this group (59 percent) as opposed to 90 percent with Silents and 85 percent with Boomers, should really be alarming to Republican honchos. Those kinds of numbers, if replicated with other age groups, would spell partywide doom of the sort not seen in a long generation. And it's already happening: Pew found in 2017 that nearly a quarter of young Republicans were so repulsed by President Trump that they left the Republican Party altogether.[10]

Why? The national Republican Party seems set to continue galloping off the far-right edge of the ideological spectrum in years to come. The most prominent and powerful Republicans of the Trump era—people like Lindsey Graham and Tom Cotton and Josh Hawley and Marcia Blackburn—are either young, or young enough to stay in power for another decade. The party's base is, more so than ever before, elderly and white and firmly entrenched in climate denialism, racial panic, and culture war hysteria. The party's discursive model is increasingly dependent on the ability of *Fox News* and One America News (OAN) to launder absurdities for their audiences and to unify viewers and, importantly, writers and analysts around a set of talking points and rhetorical strategies. All cable news viewership is dominated by older Americans, meaning that this shrinking base of slowly dying white people will be ever more mind-warped by the dictates of their broadcast overlords and whatever it is that they want their viewers to do or so or believe or vote for.

But young Republicans, like young people all over the country, do not watch cable news, just one more insane and destructive habit that America's youngest humans may ultimately rid us of. Pew found that 58 percent of Americans sixty-five or older "often" get their news from cable networks like MSNBC, CNN, and Fox. That number is only 10 percent for eighteen-to-twenty-nine-year-old conservatives. This is particularly important because Republicans who watch Fox News tend to fall to the right of other Republicans on a wide variety of issue-areas. Forty-eight percent of Fox viewers, for instance, described themselves as "very conservative," as opposed to just 30 percent of those who don't watch the channel. Forty-three percent of Fox viewers supported a wealth tax on individuals with more than $100 million, as opposed to 53 percent support from people who don't watch.[11] Fox watchers were 12 percent more likely to say that "people are much too easily offended," in response to a question about political correctness. This tendency is clear across just about any politically salient issue you can think of. If you watch Fox, you're harder right, and if you don't, you are more moderate.

This isn't just selection effects—scholars have found that Fox has a significant and unidirectional effect on electoral choices. A 2007 study found that Fox convinced between 3 and 28 percent of its viewers to vote Republican in the 2000 election.[12] They also estimate that the increasing popularity and availability of *Fox News* added more than 6 points to the Republican vote share in the 2008 election and more than 3 points in 2004—more than enough to flip the election from John Kerry to George W. Bush. The network's power is so ubiquitous that it has inspired countless younger Americans to recount the story of how Fox radicalized their parents or grandparents, like Jen Senko in the documentary, *The Brainwashing of My Dad*.[13] During the Trump Administration, *Fox News* is credited with holding together the president's coalition by forwarding alternate-reality theories about, for example, Ukrainian interference in the 2016 election and the origins of the Mueller/Russia investigation in a supposed Obama-controlled "deep state." They relentlessly frame the news of the day in terms friendlier to Trump and Republicans than other networks. The simple act of taking a snapshot of headlines or chyrons on CNN versus Fox has become a cottage industry on Twitter.

For Republican strategists, the point is that if the party's hold on its rank-and-file depends in some way on what happens on Fox, and the youngest Republicans aren't watching Fox at all, they have a problem on their hands. The entire right-wing media ecosystem is driven by Silents and boomers sitting on top of stacks of cash who have the money to pay for Fox, the time to watch and endure it, and some scratch left over to buy Donald Trump Jr.'s book as well whatever right-wing publishers like Regnery are pumping out. What happens when young Republicans cause that whole internal conservative economy to crash? What if no one wants to go on cruises with the staff of *The National Review* and pulls the plug on cable and watches prestige TV and satire shows but simply tunes out the cable news outrage machine?

Think of it this way. If the transformation of the Silent Generation into solidly Republican involved a gradual, decades-long process of older Americans realizing that national Democrats no longer shared their revanchist attitudes about race and culture, is not the same process possible, or even likely for more liberal young Republicans? If the national party continues to move right or even just settles for the ideological positions of the Trump administration, it is likely not just to continue getting crushed with Gen Zers overall, but also to begin bleeding out Republican support in this cohort to a Democratic Party which better reflects their views on government interventionism, climate change and race relations. As millennials and Generation Z become larger and larger blocs of the electorate, the Republican Party's bare survival depends on not suffering further losses with this already heavily Democratic cohort.

That seems, frankly, unlikely based on the data that we have. If roughly a quarter of young Republicans disapprove of President Trump's performance, and more than a third dislike his stewardship of the economy, and 39 percent disapprove of his handling of climate change, how likely are they going to be to stay in the party? What that feels like is a group of young Republicans who inherited their parents' partisanship and who are going to be particularly susceptible to environmental influences on their ideology over time. To keep these kinds of voters in the fold in the long run, either the party will have to change or else these voters will have to adjust their policy views to fit the cues party elites are giving them.

Perhaps a long series of defeats will finally break the fever in the Republican Party. But in the short term and probably even the medium term, victory for the Democrats in 2020 or 2022 involves obliterating the remaining Republican moderates in the Senate, like Cory Gardner (Colorado), Susan Collins (Maine), and Lisa Murkowski (Alaska). There are few remaining moderates left in the House Republican caucus, and the ones still there are rapidly choosing retirement over a monotonous, joyless life of defending Trump and getting outvoted by Nancy Pelosi's Democrats. If Trump is defeated in 2020, he's not going to do normal former-president stuff like start a foundation like Clinton and Obama, retire to his hometown like Jimmy Carter, or quietly take up painting while contemplating the catastrophe of his time in office like George W. Bush. On the contrary, assuming he remains alive (no guarantee, judging from how he looks and sounds on any given day) former President Trump will be exerting his malign influence on the Republican Party for years to come. And if it isn't him it will be one of his hapless children, most likely Don Jr. As is often the case, even if party elders make an effort to diagnose what went wrong, they will draw the wrong conclusions. Many Republicans will conclude that Trump wasn't radical *enough*.

It's important to remember that even if Republicans are outnumbered 2–1 in the under-twenty-nine set, you're still talking about a lot of people. Millions of people. There are roughly fifty million Americans between the ages of eighteen and twenty-nine alive today. Even if just a third of them are Republicans, that's more than sixteen million baby conservatives. People who pay actual money for books written by Charlie Kirk, typically featuring posed shots of the author himself. (There are actually four separate shots of Kirk on the cover of *Campus Battlefield*, which is amazing because he looks like someone playing Alex P. Keaton in a high school musical version of *Family Ties*.) That's enough people to keep the careers of Kirk and Lahren alive and prosperous for several more decades. Many of these young conservatives are likely clustered together geographically in rural areas and outer-ring suburbs or attending Liberty or Hillsdale. Like so many of us who are surrounded almost exclusively by ideological and political comrades, young conservatives almost certainly do not realize the exact shape of their plight. In Trump's America, they likely believe themselves and their ideology to be ascendant, rather believe than the reality, which is that Trump and Trumpism are the death rattle of a rapidly vanishing political coalition. The loudest and most prominent of those young conservatives are going to be the kind of extremely online political activists who are most unrepresentative of the overall cohort, reinforcing the sense that this kind of "own-the-libs-and-drink-their-tears" conservatism is on the rise, that it has national appeal, that it can successfully contest and win national elections.

CHAPTER 6

IS THERE ANY WAY THE KIDS WON'T ALWAYS BE LEFT?

SO BEFORE YOU go betting your life savings on the next six elections like you're clairvoyant Bif with the sports book in *Back to the Future II*, there are a few things that actually could interfere with the unfolding of the GOP's nightmare scenario and prevent the realignment of American politics. While there is now roughly a thirty-five-year-long, left-leaning uber-generation moving its way through American politics and very much on the verge of upending so many of our stale assumptions and electoral outcomes, there is no law that says this must continue indefinitely. If you asked observers what they thought the shape of American politics would be after LBJ's obliteration of conservative Republican Barry Goldwater in 1964, few would have replied that young people would soon turn decisively to the right, form the backbone of several stalwartly right-wing generations and spend the rest of their miserable lives trying to screw their own grandchildren out of their chance at a decent life.

First, let's review what we know about the kids and their leftiness. Since the 2004 presidential election, voters under the age of twenty-nine have voted more Democratic than the electorate as a whole, by at least 12 and as many as 27 points in the most recent national election in 2018. While this seems intuitively unsurprising to most people, it is without any precedent in the history of American elections in the exit polling era which began in earnest in 1948. And not to insult your intelligence, but these are not the same voters in every election between 2004 and 2018. An eighteen-year-old Kerry voter in 2004 is now a married thirty-three-year-old with a mortgage and a baby. And if anything, the problem is escalating for the GOP: during the first three elections of what we might think of as the millennial era, under-thirties voted 15.3 points more Democratic than the country as a whole. In the following five, the average has been 20.6. These raw numbers are problematic enough for Republicans. After hovering in the low 20s through the 2014 midterms, millennial turnout has spiked and is gradually approaching the rates of elder generations. In 2018, 42 percent of millennials showed up to vote the Republican House out of office—still below the overall 53 percent rate of the population as a whole. Perhaps more terrifyingly for Republicans, Generation Z turnout debuted at 30 percent in 2018, about 7 points higher than the first tracked turnout percentage for millennials.

IN 2020, ONE-IN-TEN ELIGIBLE VOTERS WILL BE MEMBERS OF GENERATION Z

% of eligible voters by generation

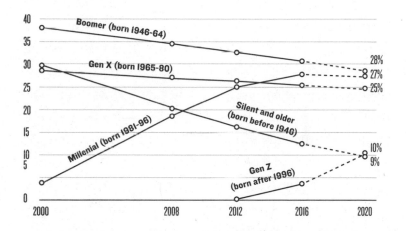

Note: Eligible voters are U.S. citizens ages 18 and older.

Source: Data from 2000 to 2016 from Pew Research Center analysis of 2000 decennial census and 2008, 2012 and 2016 American Community Survey (IPUMS). Data for 2020 from Pew Research Center projections of the electorate based on U.S. Census Bureau 2017 population projections.

The electorate changes dramatically in between our quadrennial presidential elections. We generally don't and have not really noticed because in the past there were not these kinds of extraordinary disparities in the voting patterns of outgoing and incoming generations. But the changes in the electorate just between 2016 and 2020 will be significant and deeply felt. The Silent Generation's share of the voting eligible population will plummet from 13 percent to 9 percent, and that of the boomers from 31 percent to 28 percent. While millennials will be down from 29 percent to 28 percent, Generation Z will make up fully a tenth of the electorate, up from just 4 percent in 2016.[1] That's a 12-point swing in the composition of the electorate away from the right-leaning older generations to the left-leaning younger ones. This is why the future is so grim for the GOP—having given up on appealing to young voters, the party must make further inroads with their core supporters just to hold the line against this massive demographic change. Think of it this way—if the 2020 electorate had been around in 2016, Donald Trump would have lost both the popular vote and the Electoral College decisively. We obviously don't know what the raw numbers are going to look like because we don't know what turnout will be, but there are a number of signs it's going to be very high.

Trump is a uniquely repellent figure, but the GOP's problems go far beyond him. The party's positions on social issues and climate change in particular have very limited appeal to everyone under the age of thirty. All the data we have so far on Generation Z suggests that its political and partisan attitudes are very similar to those of the millennials. And a variety of demographic factors that correlate with Republican voting—religiosity, ruralness, and whiteness in particular— are in decline with no sign of reversal. While there is some fluidity in terms of who identifies as white, most projections suggest that this will be a country without a racial majority as early as 2040.[2] Unless white Americans start voting as more of an ethnic bloc, which is very difficult to imagine given the hardened ideology and partisanship of most adults, the Republican Party is going to start losing national elections by crushing margins, and soon—perhaps as soon as 2020.

What would this look like, in practice? It's so hard for us to imagine a long period of genuine single-party dominance in American politics, because so few people alive today have experienced it. But from 1932 to 1964, Democrats won seven out of nine presidential elections and lost the 1952 and 1956 races to a man, Dwight Eisenhower, who nearly ran as a Democrat and was to the left of many of today's Blue Dogs. They controlled the Senate for thirty-two of the thirty-six years between 1932 and 1968, and the House for thirty-six of those thirty-eight years. During this period, Democrats enacted countless critical reforms, from New Deal staples like Social Security and the National Labor Relations Act to the long-delayed civil rights reforms that finally brought de jure segregation to an end in the American South.

Short story: It was not fun to be an ideologically minded Republican during this period. The outlook was so grim for so long that the center of the Republican Party moved dramatically to the left, with many in the party accepting the New Deal consensus and governing as such. Interestingly, this long Democratic Party utopia followed an extraordinarily long period of Republican dominance of national politics, with the GOP winning twelve of sixteen presidential elections between 1868 and 1928 and controlling Congress for large stretches of this sixty-year period. The lesson here is not that Democrats are going to win twelve of the next sixteen elections, but rather that the era of frequent changeovers in party control at all levels of the federal government that have characterized American politics since roughly 1992 is a huge aberration in American history. In other words, we are about to enter a period of Democratic dominance that could last for forty years—not an unreasonable assumption given that everyone born between roughly 1977 and 2006 or so leans Democratic, increasingly sharply so with those born more recently. There is no particular reason, either, to think that Americans born between 2006 and today are likely to lean Republican. It could be fifty years. And it could start in November 2020 and last until long past when most of the people holding this book in their hands are dead.

Single-party dominance isn't just a feature of American history but also of the American present—not nationally but in the states. Many US states are effectively one-party fiefdoms, with the opposition limited to nabbing the occasional governor's seat when the dominant party is in trouble nationally or when a particularly corrupt or inept regime manages to fumble power away. For Democrats, these are large states like Illinois, New York, and California, but also smaller states like Delaware and Vermont. For the GOP, Democrats are essentially a nonentity in countless states across the Deep South and plains, including Alabama, Arkansas, the Dakotas, Idaho, and Wyoming. These party alignments do shift, but they do so slowly, and it really is striking how many states now have a decisive partisan lean. If it can happen at the state level—and it does, frequently and over the long haul—there is no reason to believe that it is no longer possible nationally. And believe me, there are precious few analysts in the country who believe it is the Republican Party on the verge of a lengthy stay as the predominant party in American politics.

Why is all of this happening? The thesis of this book is that it is primarily Republican attitudes and policies that have led to the party getting crushed with everyone born after 1981, in the same way that Democratic policies at the national level eventually turned a significant number Silent Generationers into Republicans. The aftermath of the Great Recession, which left millennials in particular permanently behind in the scramble for homeownership, retirement savings, and job attainment, has hardened the political attitudes of the whole generation, and that seems unlikely to change. Because the GOP was in charge during both the Great Recession and the launching of the calamitous Iraq War, there is likely no shaking the millennial generation from its attachment to Democrats, its revulsion against Republicans, or its more general beliefs about things like taxes, foreign policy, and government intervention in the economy. Today's youngest voters, however, were only a year or two old for the Iraq War and have, at best, the dimmest memories of the Great Recession and its horrific aftermath. There has been no policy shock comparable to the terrible events of the early aughts to explain why the youngest voters today are shifting so dramatically to the left. Instead, it can only be the other factors that determine political socialization, including parental partisanship and peer group attitudes.

The latter seems particularly relevant here. The parents of Gen Zers are mostly Gen Xers. Younger Xers (like me) are a Democratic-leaning group but hardly decisively left enough to explain the aggregate views of their children. Older Xers, the parents of today's millennials youngest and some Gen Zers, are actually pretty conservative. Today's forty-eight-to-fifty-seven-year-olds have voted Republican in every national election since 1996.[3] Instead, many people in this generation are almost certainly taking their political cues from their classmates, friends and older siblings, all of whom lean decisively Democratic. Just as important, though, is the continued rightward drift of the Republican Party, which has taken a particularly ugly turn in the past decade. For the newest voters in 2020, the very first thing they remember about politics in this country is the shocking takeover of the Republican Party by a subliterate, racist, misogynist game-show host who turned national politics into a gruesome circus. They probably don't remember Merrick Garland or the fights over the debt ceiling or the battles over Obamacare or George W. Bush's epic misrule. Had Republican leaders made different choices over the past decade, they almost certainly could have wiped the slate clean with Generation Z. But they didn't. They decided to stage an unprecedented assault on the rule of law on behalf of their gangster president.

If you were being particularly charitable, you could say that Republican losses with millennials were in some part due to luck—it seems somewhat unlikely that John Kerry would have somehow avoided holding the bag for the Great Recession, seeing as how his campaign had little to nothing to say about the issues that caused it. Had President Kerry presided over the implosion of the global economy in 2007–2008, Democrats may have lost the 2008 election and taken a significantly larger share of the blame for what transpired, in ways that might have had a lasting impact on millennial voting patterns. But the GOP's troubles with Generation Z cannot be blamed on the vicissitudes of economic recessions or on a single calamitous foreign policy mistake. Instead, it is the policy stances of the national Republican Party today which are so thoroughly turning off young folks. Overwhelming majorities of young Americans want the government to do certain things, like forgive student loan debt, aggressively fight climate change, and ensure that all Americans have access to affordable health care. The national Republican Party wants to do the opposite.

The GOP's losses with the youngest voters are so staggering and incomprehensible especially because the economy under President Trump has been quite good until the COVID-19 viral pandemic erased years of employment and stock market gains. While the larger structural problems that have plagued the economy for many years are still there—too much personal debt, spiraling housing prices, relatively stagnant wages in the face of inflation, and especially inflation in key goods like health care and education—the top-line numbers had been quite good until the coronavirus unleashed its hellish fury on the economy. Young voters, instead, are rejecting the GOP's incessant culture war along with the Trump administration's attempted restoration of white male hegemony over this country. The geniuses at 1600 Pennsylvania seem to think there is no cost to staffing the executive branch exclusively with elderly white men who are hostile to women's reproductive rights and racial justice, but those costs are really being felt most acutely with the youngest voters.

But that frustration isn't just emotional. It's about policy differences, with younger Americans, including even young Republicans, favoring an increased role for the government in the economy, feeling alarm at the galloping pace of climate change and what it portends for future generations, supporting equal rights for LGBTQIA Americans, and expressing more progressive views on racial issues. On each of these issues, the Republican Party is very much on the wrong side of the policy debate for young voters. And in the Trump Era, they are no longer really pretending otherwise. While previous iterations of the GOP were careful to couch their policies in the ecumenical language of American politics, President Trump and his allies make no secret of their disgust with immigrants, city-dwellers, blue-staters, Muslim Americans, Latinx, and others. Their divisive rhetoric, their insistence on dividing the country into "real Americans" and everyone else, their relentless quest to privilege white Christian priorities, beliefs, symbols, and policies over everyone else could not be more at odds with the incredibly diverse Generation Z and the even more heterogeneous cohorts to come. You can run down the list of policy preferences of the younger generations, and you would not find a single one where the Republican position is a better fit than the Democratic one.

Young voters in particular have begun to feel an acute sense of generational warfare, that the Baby Boomers profited from America's extraordinary postwar prosperity and instead of building on it and extending it to the coming generations, greedily hoovered up the houses, jobs, and capital while simultaneously gutting the capacity of states and the federal government to fund existing higher education commitments and social insurance programs, let alone to expand them to anything resembling Western European levels. This broad sense of frustration that their elders are selfishly hoarding resources and spiking inequality to previously unimaginable highs has fueled the viral "OK, boomer" meme. "OK, Boomer" means, in shorthand, that young people have become not just skeptical but contemptuous of the received conventional wisdom of older Americans. They are tired of being told what they can't afford while a few dozen people suck up half the wealth of the whole planet. They are tired of boomers and Silents relentlessly defining the horizon of the possible downward, all the while pursuing policies designed to plunge the Earth into worst-case climate change scenarios to protect the wealth and privilege of a tiny elite.

To make matters worse for Republicans, the long period of conservative, free-market economic policy that began with the Reagan presidency really does seem to have made the younger generations worse off. In 1989, when the average baby boomer was thirty-five, boomers collectively owned 21 percent of national wealth. In 2008, when the average Xer was thirty-five, their generation owned 8 percent. Today's millennials, now at an average age of thirty-two, own just 3 percent of national wealth.[4] In 1989, earlier generations were worth just four times what boomers were worth. Today, boomers are alone are worth twenty times what millennials are. Add in the Silents, and it's nearly thirty times. There are pretty easy answers for this catastrophe—boomer policymakers withdrew state subsidies for things like higher education just as costs were skyrocketing and supervised the gutting of unions, leaving non-college-educated workers substantially worse off. Boomers were also the central political force preventing America from addressing its incredible health care crisis, which disproportionately burdens the sickest Americans with debt and reduced spending power. The explosion of millennial debt has destroyed a whole generation's ability to acquire property and investments. In so many ways, this brutal economic world that millennials and Gen Zers inhabit today was created by their elders. And they know it.

For Republicans, it's going to be very hard to win elections like that once these younger people get older and start voting in more substantial numbers. With only two major parties, it is, of course, always possible for Democrats and Republicans to win when things go badly enough for their opponents. But in the long run, Republicans are going to have trouble staying in power pushing a set of policy positions and cultural attitudes that are repellent to young people by roughly a 2–1 margin.

Is there anything that might change this trajectory, and derail the coming era of Democratic dominance? Unfortunately, yes.

The first is America's miserable, archaic political institutions. As I noted earlier, the United States already has a narrow but consistent Democratic majority—and has for some time. Yet our political institutions, including in particular the Electoral College and the US Senate, are uniquely terrible at translating majority sentiment into the resulting and expected governing majorities. Twice this century, the popular vote loser for the presidency has taken office and used his power to staff other institutions of US government with right-wing ideologues, most importantly the federal judiciary. Supreme Court analyst Ian Milhiser calls federal judges "the most consequential policymakers in the nation."[5] As of this writing, President Trump has appointed a quarter of all appellate court judges—the last step before the Supreme Court—and is filling such vacancies at twice the rate as President Obama. He has already appointed two Supreme Court justices, and if the ailing Ruth Bader Ginsburg cannot survive until at least January 2021, Trump will become the first president to appoint three justices in a single term since Ronald Reagan's second term, and conservatives would then enjoy a 6–3 majority sufficient to achieve just about any Republican policy goal. That majority could intervene in a contested election on behalf of the Republican candidate, but more importantly could thwart the policy aims of the next Democratic president. If that president sees his or her policy initiatives struck down repeatedly by the Supreme Court, it could easily demoralize the Democratic voting coalition and lead to the election of another Republican. For that reason and many others, should Democrats capture Congress and the presidency this year, they must consider enlarging the Supreme Court as well as the whole federal judiciary, not just to protect existing policy achievements threatened by a hard-right court, but also to ensure that new policies are not struck down on spurious grounds.

The United States Senate will remain for some time to come as the chief obstacle to progress. The Constitution's provision that each state be represented by the same two senators, regardless of the size of the population, means that the US Senate suffers from the worst malapportionment (a measure of equal representation in legislative bodies) in the whole world. That's a small-d democratic problem, essentially impossibly to justify with any thoughtful theory, which is compounded by the fact that the current distribution of the

US population severely disadvantages Democrats in the upper chamber. The Senate is already tilted, significantly if not overwhelmingly, against Democrats. As of this writing, there are about twenty-eight Republican-leaning states and twenty-two Democratic-leaning ones. All else being equal, in a neutral political environment, you would expect the GOP to control the Senate more often than not. While Team Blue might be pinning its hopes on transformations in Georgia, Texas, and Arizona to even out the playing field, it is just as likely that in the short term, some blue states might drift rightward, particularly those with predominantly white populations like Wisconsin, Maine, and New Hampshire. As I noted earlier, I don't think it's likely or that there's a ton of evidence for it, but it's possible. The surge of Republican governors elected across New England this decade really should be the same kind of canary-in-a-coal-mine that Scott Walker's three straight victories in Wisconsin should have been prior to the 2016 election. So even if Democrats get their long-awaited leg up in Texas, which will make presidential elections basically uncompetitive for the foreseeable future, it might not fix the issue in the Senate.

Other demographic changes at least create some uncertainty for the prospects of long-term Democratic power. The most important is the ongoing population movement away from the country's interior to thriving coastal states like North Carolina, Florida, and California. According to Census Bureau estimations of each state's population in 2040, close to 50 percent of the US population will live in just eight states—California, Illinois, Georgia, Florida, Texas, New York, North Carolina, and Pennsylvania. Another eight—Ohio, New Jersey, Colorado, Arizona, Massachusetts, Michigan, Virginia, and Washington—will host 20 percent of the population. What this means, in the aggregate, is that sixteen states with 70 percent of the population will have thirty-two Senators and thirty-four states with just 30 percent of the total population will have sixty-eight Senators.[6]

Think of it this way—in 2016, those sixteen states provided 163 of Hillary Clinton's 232 Electoral votes.[7] Only four of those sixteen states seem to be trending Republican—Michigan, Pennsylvania, Florida, and Ohio at least appear to have been a very 2016-specific mirage. By 2040, thirteen or fourteen of these sixteen states could be Democratic, giving the party a massive structural advantage in presidential elections through the Electoral College but posing a genuine dilemma in the US Senate. Of the top sixteen states, the partisan breakdown in the Senate today is 20 Democrats and 10 Republicans. In the other thirty-four states, the breakdown is a terrifying 42 Republicans versus 26 Democrats. Democrats hold nearly as many seats in the top sixteen states as they do in the next thirty-four. Republicans are not stupid—they know the Senate represents their best chance of clinging to some share of national power during the coming era, and given the way enduring progress requires seizing both branches of Congress and the presidency at the same time, a Republican-led Senate could be the chief obstacle to the future power of millennials and Gen Zers.

As Todd Tucker notes in an important report for the Roosevelt Institute, "the Senate's internationally unique veto power—when coupled with the various specific inequities of who is represented and how—produce fundamental obstacles to needed structural change."[8] For most of its history, in fact, the Senate's political imbalances have helped produced considerably less progressive policies than could have been passed. The time for deference to the Senate's death grip on American politics has long since passed. That's why the next unified Democratic government in Washington must act, and quickly, to rectify this imbalance. As I recommended two years ago in my book, *It's Time to Fight Dirty*, Democrats should move quickly to admit Washington, DC, and Puerto Rico as the fifty-first and fifty-second states, which would almost certainly send four Democrats to DC under normal circumstances. State and party leaders should also consider breaking the Democratic monolith of California into seven pieces, granting Senate representation to Native Americans and even inviting far-flung territories like the US Virgin Islands into the union as states. Together with the maturation of millennials and Gen Zers into electoral forces in many states, the Senate could easily be transformed from obstacle to progress to progressive stronghold.

Yet too many Democratic elites still seem incapable of reckoning with these structural problems. It is not even clear that DC statehood—a complete layup in terms of moral and democratic justification—commands enough votes in the Democratic caucus should the party recapture the Senate this year. Discussing DC and Puerto Rico statehood in front of reporters in 2018, Rhode Island Senator Sheldon Whitehouse remarked, "You get concerns like, who do [Republicans] find, where they can get an offsetting addition to the states."[9] A disturbing number of veteran Democratic senators still believe in the fanciful "return to normal" hypothesis, by which elected Republicans will recommit themselves to America's tarnished norms, work with Democrats to enact important legislation in a bipartisan fashion, and retreat from the bare-knuckle political trench warfare that GOP partisans have been waging for nearly thirty years now. Even leading progressive candidates like Vermont Senator Bernie Sanders, as of this writing, won't commit himself to eliminating the antidemocratic, antimajoritarian filibuster in the Senate, which requires sixty votes to pass even routine legislation in the upper chamber. It looks like even the best-case scenario in November, a Democratic takeover of Congress and the presidency, will be hobbled from the start by party elites who refuse to countenance even modest acts of procedural escalation aimed at compensating for the deranged failure of our institutions to reflect the popular will.

A second danger to the progressive project is that Republicans will realize what is about to happen to them, and instead of yielding power to the opposition, will chip away at America's democratic institutions until the country no longer functions as a representative democracy but as more of what scholars call an *illiberal democracy* or *hybrid regime*. Steve Levitsky (who would later coauthor the much-discussed *How Democracies Die*) and Lucan Way defined this particular kind of country as "civilian regimes in which formal democratic institutions exist and are widely viewed as the primary means gaining power, but in which incumbents' abuse of the state places them at a significant advantage vis-à-vis their opponent."[10] Such abuses might include stacking the courts with corrupt allies who always rule in favor of the governing elite, brazen manipulation of electoral rules to benefit incumbents, electoral violence to discourage turnout, state control of media operations to deny opposition figures the oxygen they need to compete, and more. The end result is a country that still has the bells and whistles of functional democracy, but where the outcome is never really in doubt. The opposition is playing a rigged game.

This is actually already happening in the United States. The venerable Freedom House has produced freedom and democracy rankings for all countries for decades, on a 100-point scale, with 100 representing perfect freedom and 0 representing total autocracy. The United States, once one of the top-ranked democracies in the world, has bled out 8 points on its score in eight years, declining from 94 to 86. Its peers in terms of democratic performance are now less Denmark and Germany and more Belize and Mongolia. Key in the decision to bust the United States down a few notches have been

Republican-led efforts to manipulate the electoral system and erode voting rights, as well as the yawning inequality exacerbated by GOP tax, spending, and social welfare policies. The report notes coldly that "in recent years its democratic institutions have suffered erosion, as reflected in partisan manipulation of the electoral process, bias and dysfunction in the criminal justice system, flawed new policies on immigration and asylum seekers, and growing disparities in wealth, economic opportunity, and political influence."[11]

The most outrageous way the GOP has been transformed into a proto-authoritarian operation is the party's nationwide hostility to voting rights. Beginning in the early 2000s, Republican elites at the state level oversaw the passage of nearly identical laws requiring voters to present a valid photo ID in order to vote. While these laws make some intrinsic sense to voters, they have the undeniable effect of driving down turnout among Democratic constituencies, like African Americans and students. The impact of these laws is not in serious dispute. As one group of political scientists concluded in a 2018 study, "strict voter ID laws have a disproportionately negative effect on Latinos in general elections and on blacks, Latinos, Asian Americans, and multi-racial Americans in primary elections."[12]

As concerning as the Republican Party's embrace of antidemocratic tactics and laws, which has obviously accelerated in recent years, is President Trump's decision to place the party firmly in the orbit of right-wing authoritarian movements around the world. Once upon a time, US alliances with right-wing dictatorships could be explained by Cold War politics and the need to prevent such countries from falling into the Soviet camp. These justifications were always self-serving and mostly unconvincing, but it's telling that the GOP's growing affiliation with soft dictatorships like Recep Tayyip Erdogan's Turkey and Victor Orban's Hungary as well as more ruthless authoritarian governments like Vladimir Putin's in Russia is not driven by any strategic calculations about American foreign policy but more by ideological affinity. Republicans don't need authoritarian-leaning figures like Rodrigo Duterte of the Philippines to achieve any tangible foreign-policy goal. They just like them and admire them and openly yearn to bring their brand of aggressive antiliberalism stateside. Broad-daylight manipulations of election rules and procedures, like the massive purge of more than 500,000 voters in Georgia prior to the 2018 midterms, are more than just evidence that US democracy is in decline—they are proof that one of its two venerable political parties sees these antidemocratic maneuvers as the only way to preserve its unearned power in the US political system.

The only comparable instance to what is about to happen in the electorate in American history was the enfranchisement of newly freed slaves in the US South after the Civil War, which threatened the nearly one-hundred-year-long grip that the American South had on the US political system. So Democrats and white supremacists collaborated to erect a century-long system of brutal authoritarianism which deprived most formerly enslaved persons and their descendants of voting rights, economic mobility and justice until the 1960s. The irony, of course, is that America remained, from top to bottom, such a profoundly racist place that they probably had less to fear than they thought. Open white supremacy remained a viable electoral strategy clear through the present day. The institution of apartheid across the former Confederacy was implemented with the full knowledge and acquiescence of the national Republican Party and wasn't meaningfully challenged until the 1950s. There was no ideological principle at stake other than naked racism. This system remained in place even while, as noted earlier, Republicans enjoyed a long period of electoral dominance after the Civil War.

What this history should tell us is that Americans in the past have been perfectly willing to torch democracy and all of its hallowed principles even when their power was barely threatened at all. The coming ultra-generation of left-leaning American voters will threaten the core features of Republican power like no movement in the history of the American experiment: it will threaten the sordid nexus of economic oligarchy, white supremacy. It will threaten to bury the cultural right for good. And it will threaten to alter the sustaining features of American inequality, such as disparities in education funding, the transmission of limitless intergenerational wealth, the debt-industrial complex, the waste of trillions of dollars in needless military expenditures and overseas adventurism, and the corporate enrichment schemes that are the real drivers of climate change. To think that the rich and powerful and entrenched are going to give up these perks and privileges without a fight or go quietly after an electoral defeat rather strains credibility. In their hearts, many Trump supporters are secret authoritarians who yearn to start tossing leftists out of helicopters and rehoming their children with regime stooges, like during the good old days of Latin American juntas in the 1970s and 1980s. With leading Republicans inexplicably refusing the pleas of intelligence and election security professionals to prevent vote sabotage, it is not unimaginable to picture the GOP collaborating with foreign actors to steal an election in the near future—not just to ratfuck their opponents and shut down polling places in black neighborhoods and purge voters from the rolls and require poor people to show six kinds of ID to vote but rather changing the actual vote tallies and awarding power to the people that lost rather than won.

Another potential pitfall, ironically, is climate change itself. Earth has only experienced the leading edge of the changes that will be ushered in my anthropogenic warming, and thus far we have not coped especially well, politically, with any of them. But we must brace ourselves, most importantly, for waves of climate refugees who will be forced from their homes on the coasts of fragile and poor societies like

Bangladesh and Nigeria. About 650 million people worldwide live in coastal areas that will be submerged by 2100.[13] And of course, many of them will be on the move years before the last rooftop disappears under the ocean, entire island societies emptied out and their populations deposited haphazardly elsewhere. Many millions more will flee areas that have become too hot or too frequently pummeled by a variety of natural disasters. In the United States alone, there are now expected to be thirteen million people internally displaced by these processes by the end of the century, with millions more living precarious lives in places others have long ago abandoned. Indeed, the movement of people out of the American Southeast and Southwest could reorder the American political map in ways that we can scarcely imagine today.

But these dynamics are likely to be many times worse globally. Beyond the tragic human cost of refugee flows, we must also reckon with the way that even limited forced migration patterns distorted politics in Europe and North America this past decade. The collapse of Syria, a comparatively small country of about twenty-three million people, and the movement of a few million Syrians into Europe precipitated a decade-long political crisis and the rise of far-right populist parties across the continent. While few of these organizations were able to gain and maintain power outside of Eastern Europe, their newfound relevance in places like Germany and France is a disturbing omen about how wealthy societies may deal with climate refugees. And while the precise effects of the refugee crisis were different in each country, there is no question that these relatively small population movements dominated European politics for years even after the worst was over.

Enormous population movements are unquestionably adverse events. A substantial body of political science research suggests that large refugee flows can destabilize host societies, and lead to civil wars and genocides, even in those countries with the best of intentions.[14] Without descending too deeply into this specialized literature, there are a few important takeaways. First, the risk is greater in countries with limited capacity, meaning the government's general competence in providing public goods in ordinary times. Poorer countries and those with existing ethno-religious conflicts are particularly challenged by the sudden arrival of hundreds of thousands or millions of desperate people from a neighboring state. If refugees are predominantly members of a different religion or ethnicity than that of the host state, or if they could conceivably alter a delicate ethnoreligious balance, the risk is higher. Of course, refugees are much more likely to be victims of violence and persecution than they are to trigger it. And some states, even poor ones, are able to manage refugee flows competently and humanely without causing internal turmoil or exposing vulnerable people to further violence. Jordan, for example, has hosted Syrian refugee camps since 2011 so large that they would be among the largest cities in the country, and yet there has been no destabilization of Jordan itself.

In a decade or two, we may live in a world where wealthier states are asked to absorb wave after wave of climate refugees, in a context in which they are already struggling with their own climate-caused challenges. In 2017 alone, climate-fueled hurricane, wildfire and heat calamities inflicted $306 billion of damage in the United States. And President Trump was elected, in part, on a mean-spirited promise to close America's doors to desperate refugees. In the midst of a prolonged economic crisis, one either caused or exacerbated by climate-related damage, can anyone say for certain that our politics might take on a darker hue, as individual Americans seek to blame others for accelerating material decline and hardship? Damon Linker, my colleague at *The Week*, mused last year that climate change might not just strain the capacity of governments and wreak havoc on the world's most vulnerable populations, but destroy liberal democracy itself. That's because "when economic pessimism rises, hope for the future wanes, and faith in progress dies out, politics becomes darker, with anger, blame, and bitterness taking the place of contentment."[15] While it is possible that younger generations will rise to the call for action made by today's young activists, like Greta Thunberg, it is equally likely that even people who understand the causes of climate change as well as what needs to be done to fight it will recoil when asked to make the actual day-to-day sacrifices. It's one thing to yell about how "we only have ten years" on Twitter; it's another to turn off the air-conditioning for several hours a day in July.

It also matters who is holding the bag when the stochastic effects of climate change disaster are felt most acutely. There is also a fairly extensive body of political science research that suggests there are some limited electoral effects of natural disasters and that generally they are not positive for incumbent parties and politicians. While Barack Obama may have benefitted from (or at least not been hurt by) Hurricane Sandy striking just before the 2012 presidential election, that might have been an aberration. Obama may also have benefitted from the contrast between the government's response to Sandy and its seemingly inept mobilization after Hurricane Katrina in 2005.

Democrats might also sweep to power in 2020 or 2024 and move too aggressively on policy, outstripping the ability of political, economic, and social actors to manage and implement change. Nowhere is this risk greater than with the various versions of Medicare For All promised by some of the leading contenders for the 2020 Democratic nomination. While there is a broad consensus among economists and health policy experts that the US medical system is costlier and less effective than those in Canada, the UK, or Germany, where there is a much smaller or nonexistent role for private insurance companies, there is also an uncomfortable myopia in certain corners of the left about how easy it will be to fundamentally change how things work in the US. What will happen to the existing student loan debt held by hundreds of thousands of American doctors who paid exorbitant tuition to get their degrees? What will happen to the upwards of a million people who work in the private insurance industry? What is the plan for the many hospital systems which rely on inflated costs to survive? Does the US still maintain the administrative expertise and personnel depth to administer a national Medicare scheme from DC? None of this is meant to suggest that Democrats should not pursue radical change to the health system. But if we're being honest, the details are actually really important. Democrats had trouble rolling out something as simple as a website for Obamacare's insurance exchanges in 2013. And decades of GOP looting of the public sector has left the country desperately short of competent public administrators. It is possible that the wrong president, with the wrong plan, could make a hash of the whole thing in a way that finally alienates young voters from the Democratic Party.

There is also the mirror-image risk. Imagine that someone like Joe Biden wins the 2020 Democratic nomination and brings Democratic majorities with him into both branches of Congress. Instead of aggressively passing climate change legislation and working with other countries to update and expand the Paris Accords, the Biden administration pursues some limp set of reforms—modest new emissions standards, a couple of half-assed, high-speed rail systems that don't do anything to change American car culture—and fails to allocate the kind of research money that scientists need to innovate their way out of some of climate change's worst conundrums.

In that scenario, young voters may revolt against the Democratic Party because it isn't left enough, flocking to third parties or perhaps exiting the political arena altogether, having lost hope that normal politics is up to the task of arresting global warming, reversing inequality and increasing social justice. Worse, Biden's naïve faith that his Republican counterparts will come around and work with him leads him to waste precious months of his presidency trying to build bipartisan support for his public option health-care plan and the sweeping set of good governance reforms, including new voting rights protections, that the House passed in early 2019. Very little gets achieved, Democrats kick away Congress in 2022, and all of the young voters who helped put Biden into office become hopelessly cynical about the possibility of pursuing and achieving real progressive change.

While Democrats should be thrilled with most of the data we have on America's youngest voters, there is one discomfiting fact: young progressives and liberals are not especially committed to the Democratic Party itself. In the spring 2019 Harvard Youth Poll, just 39 percent of young people self-identified as Democrats. And only 51 percent of them said "strong Democrat" as opposed to the 49 percent who said "not a strong Democrat." Thirty-six percent identified as Independent.[16] Young people defected to third-party candidates at the highest rate of any population group in 2016. While 97 percent of those sixty-five and over voted for Trump or Clinton, that number was just 91 percent for the eighteen-to-twenty-nine demographic. The 6 percent of young voters who defected to Libertarian Party candidate Gary Johnson and the 2 percent who went to Green Party candidate Jill Stein were probably decisive in such a narrowly decided election. Stein's vote totals alone were greater than Trump's margins in the pivotal states of Wisconsin, Pennsylvania, and Michigan. This risk is not idle—I spent a lot of time earlier in the book talking about how Democrats have a towering advantage on measures of "leaned" party identification. And that was true. But the raw numbers look dicier. In Pew's data, fully 44 percent of millennials identified as Independents, much higher than any other generation's totals.[17] While the vast majority of those independents seem to lean Democratic, they simply cannot be counted on to turn out in election after election the way that hardened partisans can be. That means Democrats will head into every election cycle with a great deal of uncertainty about how many of their core supporters in the broader eighteen-to-forty-four demographic will either not show up on election day or will defect to third-party candidates.

I am a huge proponent of multiparty democracy, and in my last book I recommended that Democrats institute ranked-choice voting for House, Senate, and presidential elections. By allowing voters to cast the ballot of their heart, while preventing the Ralph Nader/Jill Stein spoiler effect, RCV promises to transform American democracy and inaugurate an era of multiparty democracy in Congress. And I wholeheartedly agree with Lee Drutman, who wrote in his recent book that "multiparty democracies have consistently generated stable, moderate, compromise-oriented policymaking; higher voter turnout; more satisfied citizens; and better representation of political and ethnic minorities."[18] But, and I can't state this strongly enough, multiple parties grafted onto the existing, winner-take-all electoral system for the House and Senate would be an absolute catastrophe for progressivism in America.

A fractured left, perhaps riven by two competing political parties, loses election after election to a unified, hard-right GOP. If this sounds implausible, you need to just turn your lonely eyes to the north in Canada, where parties of the left seem to enjoy something like a 60–40 advantage over parties of the right, yet nearly turned power back over to the Conservative Party of Canada by splitting their votes in just enough districts in an electoral system similar to ours. If you're not one of the few Canadian politics junkies in the United States, another example might feel more relevant. In late 2019, the United Kingdom elected the Conservative Party's Boris Johnson to a new five-year term in office. His parliamentary majority is huge, with the Tories enjoying a 365–202 seat advantage over the runner-up Labour Party. But that massive seat advantage was built with just 43 percent of the popular vote. If you add up Labour's 32.2 percent of the vote and the 11.6 percent that went to the center-left Liberal Democrats, it is more than the Tories. And that wasn't just a one-off event. Labour and the Lib-Dems (who went by many names in the past) have outpolled the Tories in every single national election since 1959, a period during which the Conservatives have ruled more often than not. Now, a specialist in British politics might try to convince me that there are real, meaningful differences between Labour and the Lib-Dems, but the reality is that they are both parties to the left of the Tories, and that the dynamics of multiple parties contested single-winner seats means that for a whole human lifetime the British left has been splitting its votes and kicking power over to a conservative party that has not for one minute enjoyed an actual majority with the voters themselves.

This is the fate that awaits America's progressives if the Sanders/AOC left peels off to form a third party, or if the party's right flank pulls a similar maneuver should Sanders or Warren end up as the nominee. If people feel strongly enough that the United States needs a third and a fourth party, they must dedicate themselves first to transforming our electoral procedures, and then to building out the apparatus of a new party. Doing the latter before the former will only lead to disaster. I sometimes fear younger voters don't really understand this.

The subtitle of this book claims that young voters will unify America—eventually. It is worth thinking for a moment about the meaning of that unity and how it might be felt and understood by future generations. Remember, of course, that even during long periods of partisan dominance of American politics, there were millions of people who sharply disagreed with the prevailing consensus—Republicans during the Great Depression who believed that the New Deal was an assault on liberty and opposed it vociferously, and liberals during the Reagan Era who believed supply-side economics was a charade and that the Republicans were generating massive inequality that might eventually erode the democratic legitimacy of the political system.

But what the leading party was able to do during those periods was define that national consensus, and force at least some level of compliance and compromise from their political adversaries. That is how the centrist New Democrats, born in the mid-1980s, dominated the politics of the Democratic Party from 1992 to 2016. By acknowledging a number of central precepts of Reaganism—that government is inefficient, that market incentives should be introduced even into sectors like air travel and public education, that the military should be venerated and generously funded, that high crime is best mitigated with aggressive policing and punitive new laws—Democrats were able to win some elections during an era in which the public leaned right. That is the same way that Republicans were able to win some elections between 1952 and 1972. Eisenhower and Nixon were certainly far to the right of FDR, but they made important concessions to the New Deal consensus, and in Nixon's case, even extended it proactively.

When we talk about a unified America, what we are really envisioning is a country that has chosen a direction, that does not vacillate wildly between two visions of the public good every two to four years, giving the appearance of stagnation and putting off difficult policy choices that would have been easier and less disruptive had they been made ten or twenty years ago. An America unified under the millennial and Generation Z version of progressivism would be one in which the ideas that tax cuts pay for themselves, or that America should spend trillions of dollars protecting and exploiting the oil wealth of the Middle East are politically marginalized. These views will still be held by some large subset of American voters, but they will be treated the same way as those who objected to the tough-on-crime rhetoric in the early 1990s. They will mostly be ignored, and their views will be treated as politically toxic nationally and will survive in power only in the small number of states where Republicans might retain a long-term edge over Democrats. In this new America, bigotry against LGBTQIA Americans will still be there, but it will move underground, into coded language, and the national consensus will treat people the way that open racists were treated over the last quarter century, at least until Donald Trump stumbled on the scene.

This unified America, led by millennials and Generation Zers, will tackle the twin crises of inequality and climate change that are the two most serious obstacles to a decent human future. It will also be tasked with cleaning up whatever generation-defining mess is left behind in the aftermath of the COVID-19 pandemic. Whether they succeed or fail at those tasks could very well determine whether the future that awaits your own kids and grandkids is one of crisis, retrenchment, turmoil and war or one of prosperity, progress, peace and comity.

If you're an older, politically engaged voter—say that you're over the age of thirty-nine when this book comes out—it is also incumbent upon you to forge alliances with these young progressives, even if sometimes you might disagree with them. The most important thing that you can do to convince young people that you care about their concerns, that you take them seriously, and that you will act with regard to their future well-being and prosperity is to stop trash-talking them. Stop calling them entitled and privileged. Stop bitching about how they do nothing but stare at their phones. Stop talking casually about what terrible, insufferable people teenagers are. They can hear you. Stop saying they don't read. More so than at any time I can remember, young people are acutely aware of what old folks think of them, and they resent it, not only because it is mostly just a bunch of lazy tropes thrown around by people who are dead inside, but more importantly because they can sense that things are worse than they were when we were kids, and they want answers and solutions, not stereotyping of the people who will be forced to live through the upheavals of the coming decades by the people who created the damn problems in the first place.

Even staunch progressives of a certain age seem to feel no shame about calling young people "snowflakes" who "all got trophies" when they played sports and need their mommies and daddies to help them do their homework in college and can't do anything on their own because of the helicopter parenting that forged them. For one thing, that particular genre of obsessive parenting is mostly restricted to a certain kind of upper-middle-class elite family. For the millions of immigrants and first-generation Americans in the millennial and Z generations who are working incredibly hard to get ahead, these kinds of youth-bashing ideas are not just hateful, they make no sense at all to them. For another, these sentiments are mostly wrong. I spend dozens of hours a month with America's youngest people, and I find them unchanged in terms of how hard they work from people that I taught eighteen years ago in my first sections as a teaching assistant in graduate school. Young people are delightful and mostly untouched by the crusty cynicism that afflicts Xers and boomers.

Not just that, but young people today, particularly those outside of the Ivy League bubble, are hustling like mad just to stay above water. They're working two or three jobs to put themselves through college and face massive loan debt upon graduation. Those who don't go to college face pervasive job insecurity and lower wages. I've worked with thousands of these kinds of students in my years teaching at Roosevelt University, and mostly I am in awe of them, of their strength and determination and their resilience in the face of a political and economic system that is deeply unfair to them. I wish more of our elites in media would get out of the student cafes at Oberlin and the quads at Harvard and Yale and spend more time at universities like mine, where the vast majority of Americans actually go for their higher education. The young people they find here will not at all fit their preconceptions and prejudices.

Most of all, remember that our kids and grandkids live in the world that we made for them. We should listen to them when we make decisions about the future, hear their concerns and work with them to address the many galloping problems that threaten to ruin the project of human society in the next several hundred years. That goes for both Democrats and Republicans, Independents, and the apolitical. If by some chance you're an elderly Republican who has gritted their way through this book to the very end, the question I'd ask you is this: Why do you keep making decisions that cause despair and sadness and rage for your children and grandchildren? Why do you not listen? Why can you not change? Is it really so hard to understand that young people want to bring a different kind of world into existence than the one they inhabit today?

These are questions that all Republicans should be asking themselves. Instead, they have chosen to double down on a political rhetoric that has thoroughly alienated young people for two decades and counting, all for the sake of clinging to power for a few more years and then lording it over everyone for another generation through the Supreme Court. I have zero sympathy for them. And honestly, if they don't read this book, and they don't change, and they plunge themselves headlong into political oblivion, that's okay with me too.

Young people are coming for them, whether they realize it or not. It will be even sweeter if Republicans are surprised by it.

Just don't say no one warned them.

ACKNOWLEDGEMENTS

Writing this book would not have been possible without the support and encouragement of so many people. I would like to thank first the College of Arts & Sciences at Roosevelt University for granting me a research leave to complete the manuscript—special gratitude to Dean Bonnie Gunzenhauser, Provost Lois Becker, President Ali Malekzadeh and our Associate Provost for Research and Faculty Success, Mike Maly for trusting me with the incredible privilege of this time off. I would also like to thank Ryan Harrington at Melville House for launching this project with me, and my editor, Athena Bryan, for her work in stewarding it through all of the editing and revision stages, and Cassie Gutman for the exceptional copyedit. Heartfelt thanks are also in order for Stephanie DeLuca, the publicist at Melville House, and to the whole editorial team there for their amazing work. Any mistakes and errors are mine and mine alone.

You also need people in your corner when the path

ahead looks long. My brilliant wife, Sheerine Alemzadeh, helped push me across the finish line during particularly difficult junctures. Our one-year-old son, Anoush, provided well-timed giggles and cuddles and helped put everything in perspective for me. As always the love and backing of my wonderful parents, Ralph and Jane Faris, was critical. Extra thanks to them, and for my big brother Jason Faris for allowing me to write about them as part of the book. Many thanks as well to my sister-in-law Katie Faris, my mother in law Yassi Habibollahi, my father-in-law Mehdi Alemzadeh and my sister-in-law Mina Alemzadeh for their love, support and encouragement.

INTRODUCTION The Republican Party is Screwed

1   "How Groups Voted in 2000," The Roper Center for Public
    Opinion Research, https://ropercenter.cornell.edu/how-groups-
    voted-2000.

2   Tom Hamburger and Peter Wallsten, *One Party Country: The
    Republican Plan for Dominance in the 21st Century* (Hoboken, NJ:
    John Wiley and Sons), 2006, 4.

3   John B. Judis and Ruy Teixeira, *The Emerging Democratic
    Majority*, p. 10.

4   Judis and Teixeira, *The Emerging Democratic Majority*, 71.

5   Dylan Loewe, *Permanently Blue: How Democrats Can End the
    Republican Party and Rule the Next Generation* (New York: Three
    Rivers Press, 2010), 43.

6   David Faris, "After the Landslide," *The Philadelphia City Paper*,
    June 2008.

7   I have obviously not learned my lesson.

8   Nate Cohn, "Huge Turnout is Expected in 2020. So Which Party
    Would Benefit?" *New York Times*, July 15, 2019, https://www.
    nytimes.com/2019/07/15/upshot/2020-election-turnout-analysis.
    html.

9   Okay, probably not, but stay with me.

10 David Brooks, "The Coming GOP Apocalypse," *The New York
    Times*, June 3, 2019, https://www.nytimes.com/2019/06/03/
    opinion/republicans-generation-gap.html.

11 Stanley Greenberg, *RIP GOP: How the New America Is Dooming
    the Republicans* (New York: Thomas Dunne Books, 2019), 257.

12 Salena Zito and Brad Todd, *The Great Revolt: Inside the Populist Coalition Reshaping America Politics* (New York: Crown Forum, 2018), 3.

13 Sanders has consistently led polling among eighteen-to-twenty-nine-year-olds in surveys that offer crosstabs. See, for example, his 25 percent–16 percent lead over former Vice President Joe Biden and Massachusetts Senator Elizabeth Warren among the under-twenty-nine set in the fall 2019 Harvard Youth Poll. Morning Consult, which has been running a tracker of the primary since 2018, also has found Sanders has an advantage with the youngest voters. Harvard Kennedy School, Fall 2019 Harvard Youth Poll, https://iop.harvard.edu/fall-2019-poll.

CHAPTER I Polar Opposites

1 David S. Broder, "Dukakis Platform Blends Innovating, Formulized Views," *The Washington Post*, March 1, 1988, https://www.washingtonpost.com/archive/politics/1988/03/01/dukakis-platform-blends-innovative-formulized-views/c60e0e87-d515-483f-b4c0-938c25f64f0a/.

2 This remains the most insane question any candidate has ever received at a presidential debate. Imagine being Kitty Dukakis watching that debate.

3 "Presidential Candidates Debate," C-SPAN, October 13, 1988, https://www.c-span.org/video/?4256-1/1988-presidential-candidates-debate.

4 Matthew Flinders, *Defending Politics: Why Democracy Matters in the Twenty-First Century* (Oxford: Oxford University Press, 2012), 40.

5 Andrew Prokop, "Here's How Many Republicans Don't Want Their Kids to Marry Democrats," *Vox*, September 23, 2014, https://www.vox.com/xpress/2014/9/23/6828715/heres-how-many-republicans-dont-want-their-kids-to-marry-democrats.

6 If you're interested in the ingredients that go into this stew, you should check out their website, which carries an explanation of their methodology at www.voteview.com/about.

7 Isaac Stanley-Becker, "'We got things done': Biden recalls 'civility' with segregationist senators," *The Washington Post*, June 19, 2019, https://www.washingtonpost.com/nation/2019/06/19/joe-biden-james-eastland-herman-talmadge-segregationists-civility/.

8 Glenn Kessler, "When Did Mitch McConnell Say He Wanted to Make Obama a One-Term President?" *The Washington Post*,

January 11, 2017.

9   Matt Grossman and David Hopkins, *Asymmetric Politics: Ideological Republicans and Group Interest Democrats* (Oxford: Oxford University Press, 2016).

10   https://www.govtrack.us/congress/bills/statistics

11   Mark Wickham-Jones, "This 1950 Political Science Report Keeps Popping Up in the News. Here's the Story Behind It," *The Washington Post*, July 24, 2018, https://www.washingtonpost.com/news/monkey cage/wp/2018/07/24/this-1950-political-science-report-keeps-popping-up-in-the-news-heres-the-story-behind-it/.

12   Stephen Hawkins, Daniel Yudkin, Miriam Juan-Torres, and Tim Dixon, "Hidden Tribes: A Study of America's Polarized Landscape," *More in Common*, 2018: 4.

13   Lilliana Mason, *Uncivil Agreement: How Politics Became Our Identity* (Chicago: University of Chicago Press, 2018), 12.

14   Mason, *Uncivil Agreement*, 13–14.

15   Alan Abramowitz, *The Great Alignment: Race, Party Transformation and the Rise of Donald Trump* (New Haven, CT: Yale University Press, 2018).

16   Abramowitz, *The Great Alignment*.

17   CNN exit polls 2018. https://www.cnn.com/election/2018/exit-polls

18   Jesse Kelly, "America Is Over: But I Won't Let It Go without an Epic Fight," *The Federalist*, June 21, 2018, https://thefederalist.com/2018/06/21/america-wont-see-go-without-epic-fight/.

19   Kevin Baker, "Bluexit: A Modest Proposal For Separating Red States From Blue," *The New Republican*, March 9, 2017, https://newrepublic.com/article/140948/bluexit-blue-states-exit-trump-red-america. People often pick on articles like this by hate-citing them, but I want to note that this would all be 100 percent fine with me. I'm just not there yet.

20   Elaine Karmack, "Solutions to Polarization" in Nathaniel Persily, ed., *Solutions to Political Polarization in America* (New York: Cambridge University Press, 2015), 99.

21   Arend Lijphart, "Polarization and Democratization" in Nathaniel Persily, ed., *Solutions to Political Polarization in America* (New York: Cambridge University Press, 2015), 74.

22   Nathaniel Persily, "Stronger Parties As a Solution to Polarization" in Nathaniel Persily, ed., *Solutions to Political Polarization in America* (New York: Cambridge University Press, 2015), 129.

23   David Faris, *It's Time to Fight Dirty: How Democrats Can Build a Lasting Majority in American Politics* (Melville House Publishing,

2018).

24   "Hidden Tribes," p. 138.

25   Faris, *It's Time to Fight Dirty*, 131.

26   Faris, *It's Time to Fight Dirty*, 138.

CHAPTER 2 The Republican Youth Apocalypse

1   Wallace-Wells, David. *The Uninhabitable Earth: Life After Warming*. Tim Duggan Books, 2019, 27.

2   Scott Waldman, "This Is When the GOP Turned Away from Climate Change," *E&E News*, December 5, 2018, https://www.eenews.net/stories/1060108785/.

3   While Trump claimed in early January of 2020 that he is a "big believer" in climate change and that "nothing's a hoax," he is known for this kind of temporary volte face, and his policy record continues to reflect a belief that climate change is either not real or not a significant threat. See: Emma Tucker, "Trump Admits Climate Change Is Not a Hoax After Proposing Rollback of Environmental Law," *The Daily Beast*, January 9, 2020, https://www.thedailybeast.com/trump-admits-climate-change-is-not-a-hoax-after-proposing-rollback-of-environmental-law.

4   Isaac Stanley-Becker, "Trump, Pressed on the Environment in UK Visit, Says Climate Change Goes 'Both Ways, *The Washington Post*, June 5, 2019, https://www.washingtonpost.com/world/europe/trump-pressed-on-the-environment-in-uk-visit-says-climate-change-goes-both-ways/2019/06/05/77c8750c-8717-11e9-9d73-e2ba6bbf1b9b_story.html.

5   Donal Green, Bradley Palmquist, and Eric Schickler, *Partisan Hearts and Minds: Political Parties and the Social Identities of Voters* (New Haven, CT: Yale University Press, 2002), 204.

6   "An Early Look at the 2020 Electorate," Pew Research Center, January 29, 2019, https://www.pewsocialtrends.org/essay/an-early-look-at-the-2020-electorate/psdt_1-30-19_electorate2020_03/.

7   "Generation Z Looks a Lot Like Millennials on Key Social and Political Issues," Pew Research Center, January 17, 2019, https://www.pewsocialtrends.org/2019/01/17/generation-z-looks-a-lot-like-millennials-on-key-social-and-political-issues/.

8   John Cluverius and Joshua J. Dyck, "Deconstructing Popular Mythologies about Millennials and Party Identification," *The Forum* 17, no. 2 (2019): 271–294.

9   David Faris, "Vote for Hillary Clinton or Die in a Fiery Apocalypse," *Informed Comment*, September 28, 2016.

10 Brittany Sullivan, "Scholastic News® Student Vote Results Are In: Hillary Clinton Picked to Win 2016 Presidential Election," Scholastic, October 18, 2016, http://mediaroom.scholastic.com/press-release/scholastic-news-student-vote-results-are-hillary-clinton-picked-win-2016-presidential-.

11 "Presidential Vote 2 Major Parties, 1948–2016," The ANES Guide to Public Opinion and Electoral Behavior, American National Election Studies, https://electionstudies.org/resources/anes-guide/second-tables/?id=403.

12 Deborah Schildkraut, "Does the Republican Party Really Have a Young Person Problem?" The Washington Post, October 6, 2017, https://www.washingtonpost.com/news/monkey-cage/wp/2017/10/06/does-the-republican-party-really-have-a-young-person-problem/.

CHAPTER 3 The Kids Aren't Getting More Conservative

1 When we argued about politics during this time period, I often threatened to go to my university's library, take out his book, and read it back to him.

2 Daniel Oppenheimer, Exit Right: The People Who Left the Left and Reshaped the American Century (New York: Simon & Schuster, 2016), 2.

3 Oppenheimer, Exit Right, 9.

4 Dick Meyer, "How Story of 2004 Election Hinged on One Exit Poll," SFGate, December 6, 2004, https://www.sfgate.com/opinion/openforum/article/How-story-of-2004-election-hinged-on-one-exit-poll-2631497.php.

5 Freedlander, David. "An Unsettling New Theory: There is No Swing Voter." Politico, February 6th, 2020

6 Hobbs, William. "Major Life Events and the Age-Partisan Stability Association." Political Behavior, Vol. 41, No. 3. 791-814.

7 Shanto Iyengar, Tobias Konitzer, and Kent Tedin, "The Home as a Political Fortress: Family Agreement in an Era of Polarization," The Journal of Politics 80, no. 4 (September 2018): 1,326–1,338.

8 Iyengar, Konitzer, and Tedin, "The Home as a Political Fortress," 1,328.

9 The story ends happily—I met my wife on OkCupid. Together we are a gigantic cliché of what scholars call homophily. We're both heavily educated progressives from major metro regions with postgraduate degrees who ended up settled in a major city with an almost exclusively Democratic-progressive social network.

10 Amanda Williams, "The Ties That Bind: The Role of Marriage in Partisan Identification," paper presented at the Midwest Political Science Association's annual conference, 2004.

11 Iyengar, Konitzer, and Tedin, "The Home as a Political Fortress," 1334.

12 Jeffrey Lyons, "The Family and Partisan Socialization in Red and Blue America," *Political Psychology* 38, no. 2 (2017): 297–312.

13 Lyons, "The Family and Partisan Socialization in Red and Blue America," 304.

14 Alicia Adamcyzk, "Millennials Are Fleeing Big Cities for the Suburbs," CNBC, September 29, 2019, "https://www.cnbc.com/2019/09/29/millennials-are-fleeing-big-cities-for-the-suburbs.html.

15 Sabrina Tavernise and Robert Gebeloff, "Are the Suburbs Turning Democratic?" *The New York Times*, October 25, 2019, https://www.nytimes.com/2019/10/25/us/democrats-republicans-suburbs.html.

16 "Party Identification Trends, 1992–2017," Pew Research Center, March 20, 2018, https://www.people-press.org/2018/03/20/party-identification-trends-1992-2017/.

17 Jon F. Hale, "The Making of the New Democrats," *Political Science Quarterly* 110, no. 2 (Summer 1995): 207–233.

18 Hale, "The Making of the New Democrats," 219

19 "Governor Zell Miller 1992 Democratic Convention Keynote Address," July 13, 1992, Video available at C-SPAN.org, https://www.c-span.org/video/?27051-1/governor-zell-miller-1992-democratic-national-convention-keynote-address.

20 "Senator Zell Miller 2004 Republican National Convention Speech," September 1, 2004, Video available at C-SPAN.org, https://www.c-span.org/video/?c4604043/senator-zell-miller-2004-republican-national-convention-keynote-speech.

21 Ed Kilgore, "The Remarkable, Maddening Career of Zell Miller," *New York Magazine*, March 23, 2018, http://nymag.com/intelligencer/2018/03/the-remarkable-maddening-career-of-zell-miller.html.

22 This doesn't correspond precisely with Pew's definition of the Silent Generation, but it's close enough.

23 Again, because ANES doesn't define generations exactly the way Pew does, "early boomer" here means someone born between 1943 and 1958.

CHAPTER 4 The Kids Are a Nightmare for the GOP

1   Alan Abramowitz, *The Great Alignment: Race, Party Transformation, and the Rise of Donald Trump* (New Haven, CT: Yale University Press, 2018).

2   Tom Rosentiel, "Young Voters and the 2008 Election," Pew Research Center, November 13, 2008, https://www.pewresearch.org/2008/11/13/young-voters-in-the-2008-election/.

3   Tom Rosentiel, "Almost All Millennials Accept Interracial Dating and Marriage," Pew Research Center, February 1, 2010, https://www.pewresearch.org/2010/02/01/almost-all-millennials-accept-interracial-dating-and-marriage/.

4   Katie Reilly, "A Generation Gap in American Patriotism," Pew Research Center, July 3, 2013, https://www.pewresearch.org/fact-tank/2013/07/03/a-generational-gap-in-american-patriotism/.

5   The fall and spring polls ask different questions. Spring polls are not available for certain years, and I've omitted those years from the chart rather than leaving them blank.

6   "A Rising Share of Young Adults Live in Their Parents' Home," Pew Research Center, August 1, 2013, https://www.pewsocialtrends.org/2013/08/01/a-rising-share-of-young-adults-live-in-their-parents-home/.

7   Richard Fry and Anna Brown, "In a Recovering Market, Homeownership Rates Are Down Sharply for Blacks, Young Adults," Pew Research Center, December 15, 2016.

8   Richard Fry, "Young Adults, Student Debt and Economic Well Being," Pew Research Center, May 14, 2014, https://www.pewsocialtrends.org/2014/05/14/young-adults-student-debt-and-economic-well-being/.

9   Tami Luhby, "Many Millennials Are Worse Off Than Their Parents—A First in American History," *CNN*, January 11, 2020, https://www.cnn.com/2020/01/11/politics/millennials-income-stalled-upward-mobility-us/index.html.

10   Alicia Adamczyk, "Here's Why Millennials Have to Fight Harder Than Their Parents Did to Stay in the Middle Class," CNBC, April 12, 2019, https://www.cnbc.com/2019/04/12/oecd-why-millennials-are-falling-out-of-the-middle-class.html.

11   Annie Lowrey, "The Next Recession Will Destroy Millennials," *The Atlantic*, August 26, 2019, https://www.theatlantic.com/ideas/archive/2019/08/millennials-are-screwed-recession/596728/.

12   Brittany Shoot, "Make Marijuana Legal? Gen X, Millennials and Generation Z Say Yes. Most Boomers? Nope," *Fortune*, March

7, 2019, https://fortune.com/2019/03/07/marijuana-cannabis-legalization-poll-generation-x-millennials-baby-boomers/.

13 Dawson, Michael. *Behind the Mule: Race and Class in African-American Politics*. Princeton University Press, 1995.

14 Dawson, *Behind the Mule*.

15 Bialik, Kristen, "5 Facts About Blacks in the U.S." Pew Research Center, February 22nd, 2018, https://www.pewresearch.org/fact-tank/2018/02/22/5-facts-about-blacks-in-the-u-s/.

16 Hispanic and Latinx, of course, mean slightly different things. Hispanic is a term that includes Spain, whereas "Latinx" excludes Spain and includes Brazil. Because neither the Brazilian or Spanish populations of the United States are especially significant, for our purposes this is a distinction without a difference. Throughout this book, I will use "Latinx" unless referring specifically to materials which cite data about "Hispanics," i.e., census materials.

17 Antonio Flores, "2015, Hispanic Population of the US, Statistical Portrait," Pew Research Center, September 18, 2017, https://www.pewresearch.org/hispanic/2017/09/18/2015-statistical-information-on-hispanics-in-united-states/#hispanic-rising-share.

18 Sandra L. Colby and Jennifer M. Ortman, "Projections of the Size and Composition of the US Population: 2014–2060," US Department of Commerce, Economics and Statistics Administration, March 2015, 10, https://www.census.gov/content/dam/Census/library/publications/2015/demo/p25-1143.pdf.

19 Monica Escalaras, Dukhong Kim, and Kevin M. Wagner, "You Are Who You Think You Are: Linked Fate and Vote Choices Among Latino Voters," *Politics and Policy* 47, no. 5: 903–930.

20 Alan Yang and Rodolfo de la Garza, "Americanizing Latinos, Latinoizing America: The Political Consequences of Latino Incorporation, *Social Science Quarterly,* Vol. 98, Issue 2: 690-727.

21 Jens Manuel Krogstad and Antonio Flores, "Unlike Other Latinos, about Half of Cuban Voters in Florida Backed Trump," Pew Research Center, November 15, 2016, https://www.pewresearch.org/fact-tank/2016/11/15/unlike-other-latinos-about-half-of-cuban-voters-in-florida-backed-trump/.

22 "The State of the Latino Vote Going Into 2020," Latino Decisions, November 14, 2019, http://publications.unidosus.org/bitstream/handle/123456789/1996/TheStateoftheLatinoVote.pdf?sequence=1&isAllowed=y.

23 Kristen Bialikand Richard Fry, "Millennial Life: How Young

Adulthood Today Compares With Prior Generations," Pew
Research Center, February 14, 2019, https://www.pewsocialtrends
.org/essay/millennial-life-how-young-adulthood-today-compares-
with-prior-generations/.

24 "In US Decline of Christianity Continues at Rapid Pace," Pew
Research Center, October 17, 2019, https://www.pewforum.
org/2019/10/17/in-u-s-decline-of-christianity-continues-at-rapid-
pace/.

25 "Atheism Doubles among Generation Z," Barna, January 24,
2018, https://www.barna.com/research/atheism-doubles-among-
generation-z/.

26 Daniel K. Williams, *God's Own Party: The Making of the Christian
Right*, Oxford University Press, 2012, 20.

27 Jessica Martinez and Gregory A. Smith, "How the Faithful Voted:
A Preliminary 2016 Analysis," Pew Research Center, November 9,
2016.

28 Ryan Burge, "Evangelicals Show No Decline, Despite Trump
and 'Nones,'" *Christianity Today*, March 21, 2019, https://www.
christianitytoday.com/news/2019/march/evangelical-nones-
mainline-us-general-social-survey-gss.html.

29 Tara Isabella Burton, "The GOP Can't Rely on White
Evangelicals Forever," *Vox*, November 7, 2018, https://www.vox.
com/2018/11/7/18070630/white-evangelicals-turnout-midterms-
trump-2020.

CHAPTER 5 Some of the Kids Are Conservatives

1 Sadly, this book went to press before I could get my hands on what
is sure to be Kirk's magnum opus, titled *The MAGA Doctrine: The
Only Ideas That Will Win the Future*.

2 Charlie Kirk, *Campus Battlefield: How Conservatives Can WIN
the Battle on Campus and Why It Matters* (New York: Simon and
Schuster, 2018).

3 D'Souza, Dinesh, Twitter post dated June 10th, 2019, https://
twitter.com/DineshDSouza/status/1138183439922999296

4 Tomi Lahren, *Never Play Dead: How the Truth Makes You
Unstoppable* (New York: HarperCollins 2019), 10.

5 Ben Shapiro, *The Right Side of History*. (New York: Broadside
Books, 2019).

6 Shapiro, *The Right Side of History*.

7 Harvard Youth Poll, 38th Edition, Fall 2019, https://iop.harvard.
edu/fall-2019-poll.

8   "Trump Approval Holds Steady in Face of Impeachment Probe,"
     Gallup, November 20, 2019, https://news.gallup.com/poll/268493/
     trump-approval-holds-steady-face-impeachment-probe.aspx.

9   "Trump Job Approval and Economy Rating Hit Highs,"
     Quinnipiac University poll, December 16, 2019, https://poll.
     qu.edu/national/release-detail?ReleaseID=3652.

10   "Partisan Identity Is Sticky, But About 10 Percent Switched Parties
     Over the Past Year," Pew Research Center, May 17, 2017, https://
     www.people-press.org/2017/05/17/partisan-identification-is-
     sticky-but-about-10-switched-parties-over-the-past-year/.

11   John Ray, "The Fox News Bubble," Data for Progress, March 24,
     2019, https://www.dataforprogress.org/blog/2019/3/23/the-fox-
     news-bubble.

12   Stefano DellaVigna and Ethan Kaplan, "The Fox News Effect:
     Media Bias and Voting," *The Quarterly Journal of Economics*
     (August 2007): 1187–1234.

13   Jen Yamata, "How Fox News Made My Dad Crazy," *The Daily
     Beast*, April 14, 2017, https://www.thedailybeast.com/how-fox-
     news-made-my-dad-crazy.

CHAPTER 6   Is There Any Way That the Kids Won't Always be Left?

1   Cilluffo Anthony, and Fry, Richard, "An Early Look at the 2020
     Electorate," Pew Research Center, January 30th, 2019. https://
     www.pewsocialtrends.org/essay/an-early-look-at-the-2020-
     electorate/.

2   Dudley Poston, "The US White Majority Will Soon Disappear
     Forever," *The Houston Chronicle*, April 30, 2019.

3   Drew Desilver, "The Politics of American Generations. How Age
     Affects Attitudes and Voting Behavior," Pew Research Center, July
     9, 2014, https://www.pewresearch.org/fact-tank/2014/07/09/the-
     politics-of-american-generations-how-age-affects-attitudes-and-
     voting-behavior/.

4   "Distribution of Household Wealth in the US since 1989,"
     Board of Governors of the Federal Reserve System, https://
     www.federalreserve.gov/releases/z1/dataviz/dfa/distribu-
     tetable/#quarter:120;series:Npercent20worth;demographic:gener-
     ation;population:all;units:levels.

5   Ian Milhiser, "What Trump Has Done to the Courts, Explained,"
     Vox, December 19, 2019, https://www.vox.com/policy-and-poli-
     tics/2019/12/9/20962980/trump-supreme-court-federal-judges.

6   Philip Bump, "In About 20 Years, Half the Population Will Live in

8 States," *The Washington Post*, July 12, 2018, https://www.washingtonpost.com/news/politics/wp/2018/07/12/in-about-20-years-half-the-population-will-live-in-eight-states/.

7   Excluding faithless elector shenanigans.

8   Todd N. Tucker, "Fixing the Senate: Equitable and Full Representation for the 21st Century," The Roosevelt Institute, March 2019.

9   Matt Ford, "Sheldon Whitehouse's Frustrating, Illogical Remarks on D.C. Statehood," *The New Republic*, October 26, 2018, https://newrepublic.com/article/151901/sheldon-whitehouses-frustrating-illogical-remarks-dc-statehood.

10   Steve Levitsky and Lucan Way, *Competitive Authoritarianism: Hybrid Regimes After the Cold War* (New York: Cambridge University Press, 2010).

11   "The United States," *Freedom in the World 2019 country report*, Freedom House, https://freedomhouse.org/report/freedom-world/2019/united-states.

12   Zoltan Hajnal, Nazita Lajevardi, Lindsay and Nielson, "Voter Identification Laws and the Suppression of Minority Votes," *The Journal of Politics* 79, no. 2 (2017): 363–379.

13   Cara Maines, "Here's How Rising Seas Could Swallow Up These Coastal Cities," *NBC News*, May 9, 2018, https://www.nbcnews.com/mach/science/here-s-how-rising-seas-could-swallow-these-coastal-cities-ncna872466.

14   Tobias Böhmelt, Vincenzo Bove, Kristian Skrede Gleditsch, "Blame the Victims? Refugees, State Capacity and Non-State Actor Violence," *Journal of Peace Research* 56, no. 1 (January 2019): 73–87.

15   Damon Linker, "Will Climate Change Destroy Democracy?" *The Week*, May 7, 2019, https://theweek.com/articles/839648/climate-change-destroy-democracy.

16   Harvard Youth Poll, Spring 2019.

17   "Wide Gender Gap, Growing Educational Divide in Voters' Party Identification," Pew Research Center, March 20, 2018.

18   Lee Drutman, *Breaking the Two-Party Doom Loop: The Case For Multiparty Democracy in America* (Oxford: Oxford University Press, 2020), 3.

ABOUT THE AUTHOR

DAVID FARIS is the author of *It's Time To Fight Dirty* and *Dissent and Revolution in a Digital Age*. He is a regular contributor to *The Week* and an associate professor of political science at Roosevelt University in Chicago.